ısight Secondary

Insight Secondary

Assessing and Developing Self-Esteem

Elizabeth Morris

nferNelson

understanding potential

Published by nferNelson Publishing Company Ltd,
The Chiswick Centre,
414 Chiswick High Road,
London W4 5TF, UK.
Tel: 0208 996 8444

www.nfer-nelson.co.uk

nferNelson is a division of Granada Learning Limited, part of Granada plc.

Typesetting by Francis Design, Wokingham.
Printed by Ashford Colour Press, Gosport, Hampshire.

Code 0090008456   ISBN 0 7087 0356-9   2(2.05)

At-a-Glance Guide to using
Insight Secondary

This manual contains everything you need to evaluate the self-esteem of an individual student or group of students and then to design an intervention programme to enhance self-esteem based on the results of the assessment. Once you have familiarised yourself with the rationale for assessing self-esteem (Chapters 1 to 3), you may find it helpful to follow the four steps below.

Step 1: Use the photocopiable **Self-Esteem Indicator** on page 135 to assess self-esteem. From the 30 questions you will be able to obtain an overall level of the individual's self-esteem, plus three further scores that look at the three components of self-esteem:

sense of self

sense of belonging

sense of personal power.

Step 2: Use the transparent **Scoring Overlay** in the back of this manual to ensure easy and accurate scoring of the responses to the Indicator.

Step 3: Using the results of the Indicator, you can then plan how to address self-esteem building in your setting. **Three options** are presented on pages 43 and 44. Your chosen option can be implemented for the individual or group by selecting activities or programmes from pages 47 to 114.

While carrying out these activities and programmes, you may choose to use the **photocopiable worksheets** on pages 117 to 131. These are clearly numbered and referred to in the text in the same way, for example Worksheet 1 .

Step 4: Once the intervention has been completed, you can re-test with the **Self-Esteem Indicator** on page 135 to monitor both the progress the students have made in terms of self-esteem development and the effectiveness of your intervention in terms of the content and processes used.

Contents

Acknowledgements

The author would like to thank the schools and educators who took part so enthusiastically in this research, in spite of their demanding timetables:

Joy Price Bish, *Year 7 Teacher and Head of Lower School, Sandford School, Cheltenham*

Mark Croad, *English Teacher, John Kyrle High School, Ross on Wye*

Steve Palmer and Year 9 Staff, *Culverhill School, Yate*

The author would also like to thank **Lynn Boyland**, *Research Assistant,* whose time and efforts in the research programme made this manual possible.

INTRODUCTION TO ASSESSING AND DEVELOPING SELF-ESTEEM

Insight Secondary: Assessing and Developing Self-Esteem is a practical tool for anyone involved in the education of young people that enables them to assess and, where required, improve the students' self-esteem. It describes and works with three components of self-esteem – a sense of self, a sense of belonging and a sense of personal power.

This manual provides everything needed to assess and develop the self-esteem of young people and is a guide for both new and more experienced teachers or professionals working with young people. It contains an introduction to self-esteem, clear descriptions of the three main components of self-esteem, an assessment tool to measure levels of self-esteem, a chapter on how to design effective programmes to build self-esteem and, finally, a section of suggestions for activities and sample programmes that can be used in any appropriate combination when creating a self-esteem development intervention.

The central feature of *Insight Secondary* is the Self-Esteem Indicator. This assessment tool enables users to pinpoint the most vulnerable component(s) of self-esteem in a young person. With this knowledge, a focused and effective development programme can be designed and delivered for the benefit of a particular individual or a group.

The Indicator highlights varying levels of self-esteem and can be completed in two different ways:

- by a teaching professional
- by a professional and student working through it together.

Once scored the assessment clearly shows the component that is most vulnerable and the one that is strongest.

An adult completing the Self-Esteem Indicator should take less than 10 minutes. If an adult and student use it together, the adult can dictate the pace at which it is completed depending on the amount of discussion he or she wants to encourage. More information on the administration of the Indicator is given in Chapter 4.

What is self-esteem?

Many believe they know the definition of self-esteem but, when asked to articulate the concept, they find this quite hard to do. This is because there are several different components to the concept. These are:

- sense of self
- sense of belonging
- sense of personal power.

Each of these components has a different degree of relevance to each individual. One person may feel that the term 'self-esteem' refers mostly to how much they believe in themselves, others may relate it to how they feel when they are with other people, and yet others may think of it as a feeling of confidence when they tackle something new or difficult. It is an extremely personal and human experience, unique to each individual, yet common to us all.

The influence of self-esteem on an individual

Both research (see bibliography) and our own experience tell us that low self-esteem will lead to a poorer quality of life, more difficulty learning and less ability to successfully take up challenges. On the other hand, adults and children with sound self-esteem seem to do well, be more popular and are optimistic about life. They may be shaken by an event but they are resilient and capable, soon overcoming difficulties and, often, turning them into opportunities. For young people this resilience can be a life-saver, protecting them from bullying behaviour, making their learning easier because they are not anxious and easing their social relationships with teachers and peers.

Both high or low levels of self-esteem tend to work in reinforcing cycles. The young person with sound self-esteem learns more easily than an individual with low self-esteem. Esteeming students soon discover that they can tackle new concepts successfully. Their achievements are likely to be good and they will get recognition and praise for this. In turn this will increase their confidence and help them feel even better about themselves. They continue to feel positive and develop an even stronger sense of their own worth and abilities. On the other hand, their peers with low self-esteem do not do well in many of the usual learning tasks and tend to get more negative attention. Young people with low self-esteem learn to deal with that by withdrawing and not taking risks with new tasks, or by developing challenging behaviour that deflects attention away from their areas of weakness. Either way is likely to lead to yet more negative messages and further reinforcement of their low self-esteem.

Changing an individual's self-esteem

Various researchers – for instance Stanley Coopersmith, Morris Rosenberg and Nathaniel Branden (see bibliography) – have discovered that self-esteem can be influenced by many things such as a person's gender, socio-economic status, appearance and peer acceptance. Even personal events such as losing a football match may deal a short-term blow to an individual's level of self-esteem. This leads us to the realisation that self-esteem is changeable, for the better and for the worse.

Teaching professionals and adults working closely with young people, with their knowledge and understanding, are in a position to minimise some of the negative impact of social conditioning and personal disappointments. They can teach young people how to reframe their experiences and have wider perspectives, and that their value does not lie in either their conformity to social pressures or their success at every task.

This provides vital support for young people, especially males, as recent research has shown that self-esteem tends to decrease significantly in 27 per cent of boys during their teenage years (Katz, 1999). This leaves them vulnerable at an important stage in their lives, just as they need to present themselves well to prospective employers or at further education interviews.

Theories of self-esteem

The phenomenon of self-esteem has fascinated social scientists, philosophers and psychologists for at least a century. Each person who has explored the concept has attempted to articulate an all-encompassing definition, with varying degrees of success. For example:

> 'Self-esteem is the evaluation we make and maintain with regard to ourselves, expressed by an attitude of approval or disapproval and indicating the extent to which the individual believes himself to be capable, significant, successful and worthy.'

> *(Coopersmith, 1967)*

> 'Self-esteem is the conviction that we are competent and worthy of living.'

> *(Branden, 1969)*

A definition that resonates with most people who hear it is:

> 'Our self-esteem is how positively or negatively we feel about being ourselves. It is the value we place upon ourselves as a unique and valuable human "being", rather than a human "doing". It depends on how well we know ourselves, the extent to which we feel we are accepted, and on our belief that we can exert an influence over other people and the world.'

> *(Morris, 1997)*

A variety of theories of self-esteem have been developed over the last century and the definitions of the concept have varied with the theory, though all have recognised the internal nature of the phenomenon – it is how 'I' *feel* about my 'self'. The theories have come from various areas of the social sciences such as psychology, behaviourism, philosophy and sociology.

One of the most important pieces of research was conducted in 1967 by behavioural psychologist Stanley Coopersmith. The three factors that he found promoted self-esteem in children in general are:

1. Carers who love and value the child and express this.
2. Carers who set firm, fair boundaries and stick to these.
3. Carers who provide opportunities to participate in certain decision-making.

Recent research by The School of Emotional Literacy in Bristol and the web-based Self-Esteem Advisory Service has added another vital component to this list, namely:

4. Carers who provide effective, assured and competent models for the child to style his or her behaviour upon.

These factors have all been incorporated into the material in *Insight Secondary*, making it a comprehensive and up-to-date resource.

Self-esteem, therefore, is many things and is influenced by many things. One thing we do know, however, is that it is real, powerful and frequently problematic, especially for young people as they move through the educational system. We also know that students are better off if they have sound self-esteem and that we can support them to develop this by interacting with them in positive, reinforcing ways.

The three components of self-esteem assessed by the Self-Esteem Indicator

During 20 years of clinical experience, most of which has focused on self-esteem and how to successfully repair, maintain and develop it, three major components of self-esteem have been identified by the author. Each of these components:

- is a crucial part of the positive or negative self-perception we come to have about ourselves;
- influences the other two;
- is distinct in its own right.

Courses run by the author, which specifically focused on one or more of these aspects of self-esteem, consistently produced more positive results than earlier experimental courses where 'life skills' or a general look at 'feeling good' were the focus. The positive results from the courses, where the components of self-esteem were the focus, were further improved when the Self-Esteem Indicator was developed. By using the Indicator it was possible to target the components that were most vulnerable in the people within the group. This enabled the facilitators to give more focused and individualised support in the course.

Sense of self

A sense of self means having a good idea about who you are – for example, knowing and being comfortable with your likes, dislikes, strengths, vulnerabilities, preferences, temperament, feelings and needs. It involves being accepting of these strengths and limitations. It also involves being aware of and able to identify and appropriately express emotions. A typical question one might ask to gain an indication of someone's sense of self would be: 'Are you pleased and proud to be you?'.

Sense of belonging

A sense of belonging refers to how aware of and comfortable you are about being in relationships with other people. If you are supported by the inner knowledge of the connections you have, even when they are not around, you have a sense of belonging. In our society young people are usually members of several groups, for instance family, school, church, sports team or a gang of friends. Knowledge of our connections with others enables us to feel well supported and more secure in the world. It also involves having good friendship-making skills and an open, tolerant attitude towards other people. A typical question asked to assess an individual's sense of belonging would be: 'Do you know that you are missed when you are not around?'.

Sense of personal power

A sense of personal power means your inner knowledge of your ability to have an impact on the world around you. It goes beyond just knowing you are good at certain tasks (which is self-confidence). It is more concerned with knowing that you are a person who can learn, cope and make changes to things you don't like or want. It involves skills such as assertiveness, self-support and accurate self-appraisal. A question we might ask to gain an idea of someone's sense of personal power is: 'Do you believe that you can make a difference to the world around you?'.

The Self-Esteem Indicator assesses each of these components, providing a focus for anyone working with a student. Whether you want to make sure that the person maintains his or her current level of self-esteem or you want to help the person develop it more, knowing which of these areas of self-esteem is vulnerable and which is relatively strong will enable you to create a focused support programme.

For example, if you are aware, through administering the Indicator, that a particular young person has little sense of his or her relationships with others and is lacking in a sense of belonging, it is likely that that student will feel insecure and frightened at some level. This will make it harder for such students to learn the academic content of the syllabus and to make friends and socialise, which is such a vital part of developmental needs during these years. Having identified this through using the Self-Esteem Indicator and consulting the activities section of this manual, you will then have a guide as to how to create opportunities for these young people to make connections with others in safe and supportive ways, such as during project work or team activities.

Monitoring any changes in their behaviour will help you change the focus of the activities as they gain more sense of belonging, and you may then find that they are ready to develop the other affected areas of their self-esteem too.

The development of self-esteem

Babies seem to have little problem with their level of self-esteem. Infants are born with a sense of what they need and a clear biological imperative to do what they can to get it. It is only through time and their interaction with others that they begin to either struggle with their sense of self-worth or feel increasingly positive about their intrinsic value as a human being. This clearly demonstrates the importance that other people, particularly significant and powerful adults, have in the development of a child's self-esteem. Peers also have an increasing impact during the teenage years, usually even more powerful than that of the adults involved with the student. This additional impact from their social world needs to be taken into account when assessing and developing the self-esteem of young people and when designing and managing self-esteem development programmes. For example, using peer mentors or encouraging pairs and small group practice of positive behaviours will be far more effective with teenagers in building their self-esteem than an over-reliance on one-to-one work with an adult.

Although positive social interactions with their peers and adults are extremely important, so too are the interactions young people have with themselves. The power of positive and negative self-talk (the internal conversation they have with themselves to give encouragement and support), and its impact on self-esteem, has been recognised by psychologists and specialists in communication. By the time students reach their teenage years, they are theoretically almost at a point where they are able to support themselves emotionally and intellectually. Whether they actually use this capability depends on whether they have been taught and encouraged to use 'emotional literacy' techniques to help themselves (see page 8). This means that they have learnt how to give themselves encouragement and feedback rather than having to wait for some other significant person to give it to them. The increasing sense of independence they derive from using this technique also builds their self-esteem because it is directly related to their sense of personal power.

One of the processes that often takes place during the early part of children's lives is that they are given 'conditions' by which they will be judged. Adults sometimes use words that imply to children that they will not think so highly of them unless they are well behaved, happy, handsome, clever, talented, polite, pass all tests, get good reports, etc. Although in many cases this is not actually true, what is important is what the child *understands* from the adult. It can be hard for children to understand that they are loved and appreciated for their uniqueness and humanness when they hear a constant stream of wishes for them to be something else. These attributes then are the 'conditions of worth' that a child comes to associate with being accepted and acceptable to important people.

For most people, these early messages about our acceptability last into adulthood, subtly influencing our behaviour, for better or for worse. Not surprisingly, if individuals have received many of these 'conditions of worth' and little acknowledgement of their achievements and personal characteristics, they will end up with little sense of themselves as an acceptable person. This can drive them to try to impress other people in order to be accepted, or to be angry and oppositional because they are not capable of living up to the demands they believe are being placed on them. Young people may act out these feelings in their behaviour towards influential adults around them. With some teenagers this is complicated even further because, in common with many other young people, they want to free themselves from parental and adult influences and they respond to this wish by developing an opposing stance to those 'conditions'. Since the conditions of worth have been deeply ingrained in their psyches and act as drivers of many of their behaviours, it is very hard work to manage the inner conflict between this unconscious motivation and a more conscious wish to cast off these mental shackles. Their struggles with this conflict can attract ever more negative messages and turn into an unhappy, internally reinforcing cycle of feedback, constantly eroding their self-esteem.

In the activities and programmes section of this manual, a range of ways are presented that can be used within the programme delivery to convey to students that their acceptability does not only depend on their social attributes, behaviour or achievements.

The importance of self-esteem

'His self-esteem could be higher.'
'She has low self-esteem.'
'His low self-esteem lets him down.'

These phrases are becoming more and more common in school reports. Over the past ten years there has been a steadily increasing recognition that self-esteem plays a large part in students' academic results as well as in their ability to cope successfully with the social and emotional aspects of secondary school life. For example, in a study conducted by Psychology Professor John Gottman of the University of Washington (1997), children who had grown up in an esteeming environment were found to have greater popularity, be more resistant to stress, suffer fewer infections and have greater academic success in their senior school years than children who had grown up with a diet of negativity and unrealistic demands. They were more able to support themselves with affirming self-talk and less likely to use phrases such as 'I can't do that' or 'I'm stupid'. There were many other associated benefits to this too; for instance, the self-esteeming students were also far more able to handle attempts to bully them, were far less likely to have been in trouble with the police, and also less likely to have experimented with drugs or had to deal with teenage pregnancy.

This kind of research demonstrates the importance of self-esteem building, and *Insight Secondary* provides guidance for each step of the self-esteem building process.

Self-esteem and emotional intelligence

There are strong connections between self-esteem, which has been researched and described for many years, and a newer concept that has been steadily emerging over the past 15 years. This new concept is called 'emotional intelligence' and the emotional intelligence of students is now being given serious attention by teaching professionals.

'Emotional literacy', as it is more commonly called in the educational field, is the practice of being aware of, understanding and managing emotional states in both oneself and other people. This is not the same as self-esteem, which is the inner perception people have of themselves as being more or less valuable, worthy and powerful in the world. However, the connections between the two are clear. For example, it is hard to feel good about yourself if you do not know yourself well. You will only feel powerful and capable of making an impact if you can recognise and manage your own emotions, such as anger or frustration, effectively. If you are able to read body language and relate to other people and their emotional states well, you are likely to be popular and this encourages a sense of belonging.

Far from being seen as a negative influence on a person's cognitive strengths or a stimulus to very challenging behaviour, emotions are now being recognised as a potent and valuable source of information. Research carried out by Antonio Damascio (1994), a brain surgeon and neuroscientist, gave compelling evidence that it is the access to our emotional states which allows us to make decisions and plan. Without this access to the emotions, memory may remain intact, but the ability to decide what to eat, where to go, when to take a holiday and other everyday decisions will be absent. Without this decision-making capacity a person's lifestyle will disintegrate, leaving him or her dependent on other people for many things.

Other researchers have expanded our knowledge of the brain and the centrality of the emotional system within it. In particular, they have highlighted the limbic system, which carries the majority of the receptor sites for the biochemical messengers called peptides that carry emotional information around the body. The limbic system has a complex set of connections with the neo-cortex, where the majority of the cognitive processing and attention focusing takes place. These connections make it possible to integrate our thinking and feeling, which in turn leads to our being able to choose the most effective behaviour in any situation.

Just like teaching literacy in languages or computers, students can be taught how to read, comprehend and express their own emotional states and to read, comprehend and manage those of other people. Thus materials and programmes to develop emotional literacy are becoming more common in schools. This has been particularly true since psychologists Peter Salovey and Jack Meyer (1990) first coined the term 'emotional intelligence' and began to link it to abilities we have that can help us regulate our behaviour more appropriately through integrating our feelings and thinking.

If teaching professionals and adults working closely with young people develop emotional literacy in their students they will affect the students' self-esteem, and if they develop self-esteem they will also improve the level of emotional literacy: these are two sides of the same coin. The Self-Esteem Indicator can help with this, particularly by highlighting the extent of a student's sense of self. This particular component of self-esteem is strongly linked to emotional literacy and shows how well students understand and know themselves, including their emotional states.

Self-esteem and self-confidence

Another important term in the world of self-esteem building is 'self-confidence'. It is obviously linked to self-esteem, but it is not the same and it is important to make a clear distinction between these two phenomena. A crucial distinction between the two concepts is that self-esteem is what we feel about ourselves and our sense of self-worth. This is related to us as a human 'being'. Self-confidence, on the other hand, is what we feel about our capacity to do things. This is related to us as a human 'doing'. For instance, you may feel confident in your ability to teach maths to 14-year-olds but not so sure about how valuable you are as a unique human being. Another person may feel a sound sense of self-esteem, sure of themselves and their place in the world, but may not be self-confident about their ability to teach maths to 14-year-olds.

Sorting out the difference between these two concepts can be extremely helpful when you are deciding what to focus on in a young person's self-esteem development plan. In many settings, students are frequently given words of encouragement for the things they are doing (and even more frequently corrected and criticised for what they are not doing properly), but receive very little encouragement for how unique they are, how much they are valued for being in the group and for how powerful they can be. The focus in schools tends to be on building self-confidence, *not* self-esteem. Young people need both, and frequently need their self-esteem building up first, since a sound sense of self-worth promotes better learning and skills development than a low sense of self-worth.

FROM THEORY INTO PRACTICE

Chapter 1 provided the first step in this manual of developing a better understanding of what self-esteem is and what it involves. This chapter moves away from theory and introduces practical tools that can be used to assess and develop self-esteem.

Two elements to building self-esteem

There are two elements to building self-esteem in young people.

- First, there is creating a self-esteem enhancing environment.
- Second, there is delivering a specific programme to a student or group as a remedial or preventative measure. Such programmes can each have a different focus – they can be either specifically a 'self-esteem' building programme or a skills development programme which is run in such a way that it promotes self-esteem as a by-product. Of these two programme options the latter seems to work better with teenage boys. Teenage girls are not so sensitive about having 'self-esteem' building as the focus for the programme.

Ideally, a self-esteem promoting environment and a focused skills-based programme would be used together, since learning in an environment where they are valued and respected will automatically raise self-esteem in students. In either case an assessment is an invaluable tool to help the adult supporter accurately identify the areas that need support. Alternatively, it can help to establish how effective the self-esteem enhancing culture actually is.

Creating a self-esteem enhancing environment

Creating a self-esteem enhancing environment is the top level of intervention with young people. Ideally, it would be part of a whole school policy on self-esteem development. Developing self-esteem throughout the whole setting requires some knowledge and skills on the part of the teachers, and specifically the heads of year, such as active listening and focused questioning. It also requires values of respect and empathy to be held along with other typical school values such as co-operation, high standards and so on. It needs a willingness to keep on evaluating the results by using some form of assessment. For example, making some measurement of how the young people feel about themselves before instituting a whole school policy and then comparing the results one year and three years later gives very important information about the success or ineffectiveness of the policy.

Using the Self-Esteem Indicator included in this manual can rescue a well-meant, but ineffective, self-esteem policy by pinpointing the areas in which the school is not managing to support self-esteem, as well as the areas in which it has been successful. For example, many schools find it hard to help the students feel as if they individually matter in the busy and often crowded secondary school environment. Pride in being a member of that school or year group tends to be low. Having used the Indicator, the school can turn its efforts to creating activities and practices that will develop a sense of connectedness (such as the regular use of assembly time to recognise individuals, regular parent contact, developing a positive high profile for the school in the community, use of a school council, etc.), whilst continuing to do the other things that have been successful in its policy, such as encouraging a sense of self.

Designing and implementing a development programme

Designing and implementing a social and emotional development programme for individual students or a group that is suspected of having low self-esteem, which is impacting on their work and classroom behaviour, is another way to help young people. Programmes designed for this purpose often use materials such as worksheets and exercises to help the young people to get to know themselves better, to make connections with one another and to stretch their abilities. Typically, these kinds of activities take place during Personal Social and Health Education (PSHE) time or in the Citizenship Curriculum. However, this will not have the desired effect unless the activities are used in an integrated and systematic way and are focused on the areas of need most demonstrated by the group or individual.

It is vital that these programmes are carefully graded into achievable steps, each of which builds upon the one before, in order to be effective. Chapter 5 of this manual presents a checklist of critical success factors, and an example programme outline for guidance is found in the 'Activities and example programmes' section (Section 6).

Why use a self-esteem assessment?

Assessments are a crucial part of any self-esteem building intervention. They perform several functions.

First, they enable the user to establish areas of strength and areas that require intervention.

Second, they can be used to monitor progress if they are administered regularly.

These two functions enable teaching professionals and students to:

- monitor progress together, seeing which areas have changed significantly, which are beginning to change and which have remained the same;
- evaluate the appropriateness of the methods they are using together, give focused and specific feedback to one another and adjust their actions accordingly. This type of process is enormously encouraging for young people and particularly effective at building a sense of personal power.

An assessment procedure also enables professionals who are interested in evaluating the progress, results and cost-effectiveness of an intervention to monitor what is happening. This type of information is extremely useful if programmes are to be rolled out to wider groups.

Third, a good assessment tool enables a tentative 'diagnosis' to be made. From this the best and most appropriate 'remedies' can be selected to help the individual or group, thus saving time and helping the students receive the support they need as quickly as possible.

Fourth, tests can give important information about different populations of students and provide a helpful comparative guide to professionals as they work directly with students or plan strategic interventions to improve performance.

Developing a practical assessment tool

Quantitative assessment of self-esteem can be complex and has been tackled with varying degrees of success as researchers and test developers have tried to put together a test that reliably differentiates between self-esteem and other human motivational factors. Tests have tended to be lengthy and therefore difficult to administer to younger or less able students, or too inconvenient because they take so long to complete and score. Furthermore, immature teenagers are not very good at making accurate reflections about themselves and their responses. They tend to answer as they think the adult wants to hear, and this has meant that self-report tests provide little useful information. Tests that have managed to combine robust design with practicality and offer scales that discriminate are normally for use only by trained professionals such as educational psychologists.

Interestingly, most educators have a good idea which students are suffering from a lack of self-worth and low self-confidence. The students' body language, general behaviour and their interactions with adults and peers all give cues that experienced educators will pick up. For many, this subjective and intuitive assessment of a student is what they base their planning on when they are thinking of ways to work with the individual. They identify the vulnerable person and decide, for instance, to make sure that they give that individual some extra attention when in the year room, or to make a point of being around to talk to when there is a quiet working period in the subject class. This subjective form of assessment has some advantages, the first of which is speed! However, this type of assessment is not formalised enough to give a clear direction for future work.

Clearly, a tool that sits somewhere between the rigour and specialised, time-consuming nature of a standardised psychometric test and the intuitive sense of a student and his or her level of self-esteem gained by an observant, experienced educator strikes a good balance between speed, practicality and utility.

The Self-Esteem Indicator

The Self Esteem Indicator, which can be found on page 135, provides this balance. It is a tool designed purely for developmental purposes and not for statistical research. It is therefore quick to complete and easy to use. As it is built around a clear model of self-esteem and is supported by well-researched theories, the results it gives are far more focused than fleeting impressions and intuitions. This means that interventions and actions taken afterwards are based on a clearly and accurately identified need. This saves time and expense when working with students. The instructions on how to administer and score this Indicator are given in Chapter 4.

The model

The model of the three main components of self-esteem has been developed and validated by the author through careful observation of adults, teenagers and young children in various clinical practices, as well as school and workplace environments, over a period of 20 years. In Chapter 4 on administering and scoring the Self-Esteem Indicator, the three main components – sense of self, sense of belonging and sense of personal power – are explained again to help the user quickly make sense of the results.

The outcomes

The Indicator provides results on two levels.

The first is a **total score** – the *overall self-esteem score*. This figure gives a basic indication of the level of a student's self-esteem. It is divided into four ranges representing high, good, vulnerable and very low self-esteem. This score is useful for assessing whole groups when a trend to indicate the general level of self-esteem in a class is needed.

The second set of scores shows students' weakest and strongest **components of self-esteem** – the *component scores*. This is invaluable for working with individuals and small groups when the finer detail of the components of self-esteem is required.

TRIALLING OF THE SELF-ESTEEM INDICATOR AND PROGRAMME

Trialling design

The Self-Esteem Indicator has been trialled by over 100 teaching professionals in a wide variety of educational settings over the past three years. These have ranged from mainstream primary schools, to after-school clubs, to schools for children with a wide variety of special needs, to EBD units run by a local education authority. (The *Insight Series* also covers pre-school and primary settings.)

The most recent trial was conducted in three volunteer schools and the following comments were made by the teachers involved:

> 'Superb!'
> 'A good resource for the kind of work we do.'
> 'Good ideas and easy to adapt.'
> 'I like the emphasis on drama, activities and encouragement of students' thoughts, feelings and opinions.'
> 'Using the Indicator meant that almost every interaction with that young person was affected because of what I now knew.'
> 'Good for focusing in depth on a person and understanding him or her better.'

The trial aimed to find out how effective the Self-Esteem Indicator was at identifying the areas of self-esteem where a student had more or less vulnerability. A short follow-on intervention was conducted to validate the trial of the Indicator as an effective diagnostic assessment. The intervention was a programme of assertiveness training for young people, which can be found on pages 83 to 110. The rationale for using an assertiveness training programme was based on informal discussions with the schools concerned, which had pointed to the likelihood that the students' sense of personal power would be low. Therefore, an assertiveness programme that gave them the skills to use wider communication options seemed to be the best way to focus on this, while also creating opportunities for the other components of self-esteem to be explored and developed in different individuals. This informal observation regarding low personal power was confirmed by the initial assessment using the Self-Esteem Indicator.

The trial involved asking teachers and tutors to select a particular group of students with whom they wanted to work. The adults then used the Self-Esteem Indicator to assess the individuals in the group. At the time of using the assessment the teachers were taken through a semi-structured interview in which they discussed each young person in the light of four areas of educational interest, namely classroom behaviours, social behaviours, emotional responses and academic achievements. The teachers then began to use the training programme, putting time aside each week to do it as part of the PSHE Curriculum.

At the second interview, which took place after the programme had been delivered, the teachers re-assessed the students using the Indicator and were re-interviewed using the same categories to structure the information.

Results

The results in these secondary school settings for young people who were believed to have low self-esteem showed that:

- 75 per cent of the students assessed had a vulnerable or low sense of personal power;
- 16 per cent of the students assessed had a vulnerable or low sense of self;
- 9 per cent of the students assessed were equally low on all three components and fell within the low and vulnerable ranges.

These results show that three-quarters of the young people assessed had low scores for their sense of personal power. Students are being measured continually during their adolescence to ascertain their levels of competence at all kinds of tasks and, for many students, this seems to lower their sense of themselves as competent, 'can-do' people (Katz, 1999). Most students scored relatively well on their sense of belonging compared to the other components. Given that many young people are very influenced by their peer group and that it is seen as being extremely important to belong to a group, most teenagers seem to have found themselves friendships that give them some sense of self-esteem. This is in contrast to the primary and pre-school children who had far more difficulty with their sense of belonging. The sense of self was specifically problematic for one-sixth of the students assessed and, in this sample, this was more particularly true of the girls. A developmental task for teenagers is to re-assess their own identity in the light of their physical changes. Many of the students assessed seemed to be aware of this and were struggling with this aspect of recognising and understanding their emotions.

Following intervention

As a result of suggestions and input from teachers, the Self-Esteem Indicator was reduced from 36 to 30 questions for the secondary version. As a result the Indicator has become easier to complete and more focused on the specific behaviours that point to the different components of self-esteem.

Cut-off points for the overall self-esteem score were developed by dividing the score range into quartiles and monitoring the numbers of those assessed who fell into each quartile over time. The Interpretation Guide on page 21 shows these results.

In this trial, following the intervention, students tended to improve their positions on over a third of the statements. This meant that the tutors rated them one or two points higher on the four-point scale on at least 12 statements during the re-test. In some cases the students improved on as many as two-thirds of the statements, that is, they improved their rating on 20 of the 30 questions.

Changes in rating were made in statements that reflected each different component of self-esteem, not just those that had been focused upon through the activities. This reinforces the view that self-esteem influences, and is influenced by, the whole person. It is impossible to isolate one part of it and effect changes only in that part. However, an initial assessment and identification of the most vulnerable component is essential to help to focus the intervention on the area that most needs support. From previous studies we have seen that a random choice of activities can bring about some changes, but not at the level of those seen in these results.

After the initial assessment and use of the prescribed programme (assertiveness training), the students assessed showed the following changes:

- 91 per cent improved on social, emotional and classroom behaviour indicators, but not academic indicators;
- 9 per cent improved on all indicators.

The results clearly showed that the young people who were assessed and then supported by learning a helpful set of skills in a well-facilitated group environment tended to respond most powerfully through changes in their social, emotional and classroom behaviours. For example, typically this meant that they improved their capacity for empathy considerably and were far more willing and able to work as a team after this intervention. They all seemed to have more confidence in themselves, as was evident from their changed approach to tackling new tasks where their fear of failure seemed to have diminished significantly. Post-intervention assessment showed a strong improvement in their sense of personal power and anecdotal evidence from other staff members told of incidents where they used phrases they had learnt in the programme in a variety of different situations. In one case two boys discussed whether they would have a fight or sort out their differences through discussion. They decided on discussion and were able to manage this successfully without adult support.

Fewer students had changed the standard of their academic work but, out of those that had changed, several seemed to have made large improvements in the term during which the programme was delivered. All staff involved with the group commented on this and, particularly, that the students who had improved were also showing signs that they considered it 'cool' to achieve. This was a very significant change for these teenagers. One area of academic work that did improve generally was in the presentation of their work.

It is worth noting that the research also showed very clearly that students with moderate to severe emotional and behavioural difficulties did not respond well to interventions that involved only increasing the amount of praise they received. Their lack of trust was too great and their behaviour patterns too entrenched to respond positively to this. However, a different pattern of praise which included more specific constructive criticism along with a small amount of general praise was more successful. In contrast, increasing the amount of positive praise only in a mainstream classroom was effective, although teachers said it was hard work at first. In both cases the tutors commented that these types of intervention need to be given plenty of time and changes would be seen over a whole term rather than a shorter period. Without a doubt, the most effective intervention was the provision of a specific programme, such as assertiveness training, anger management, stress management or self-esteem building. This was effective in improving each component of self-esteem in a wide range of students.

The benefits of using the Self-Esteem Indicator

From the trialling, several clear benefits of using the Self-Esteem Indicator emerged.

From the teachers' and tutors' comments it was clear that the Indicator confirmed the difficulties they had noted in the students and enabled them to understand what this meant more fully. On completing the Indicator, the professionals found distinct differences emerging for each student. For example, the scores in each of the main components were different, as were the relationships between highest and lowest. Further discrimination was possible when the ratings of individual statements were examined in more detail.

On re-testing with this measure after a development intervention, the teachers were able to track changes in the scores in the main components. They were also able to give anecdotal evidence of changes in the classroom behaviour, social behaviour, emotional management and academic achievements of the young people, which corresponded to the scores in the different components of self-esteem.

The professionals recognised their own observations of the teenagers in question in the Indicator results. Thus, the Indicator provides face validity. Informal observations also revealed that there was a high degree of agreement among the people who knew the students when the Indicator was used to assess and re-assess the group. In several cases in the trial, other professionals joined in with the research as interested observers. They usually knew the students selected and were able to confirm that the scores reflected their own opinions.

From the comments of the professionals, it can be concluded that the Indicator offers a useful tool to guide their self-esteem development efforts with the students. It seemed to be helpful on different levels:

- in validating the professionals' own intuition;
- in helping to motivate both student and professional to continue with a development plan;
- in saving time by offering a focus.

ADMINISTERING AND SCORING
THE SELF-ESTEEM INDICATOR

The Indicator can be used in two ways.

1. Completed by an adult about a student

This is the best way and is the method most strongly recommended by the author since it was the way in which the assessment was designed. The language and sentence construction is most suitable for adult comprehension and refers to 'this student' throughout.

Note that some of the questions, such as 'Do you like this student?' and 'Do you feel interested/excited when you think of this student, rather than worried or annoyed?', are intended to prompt you to think about your own reactions to the individual. Even though they seem to require rather personal responses, it is important to take time to reflect for a moment and give an honest answer. This may elicit important information about the student, which may not be immediately obvious: for example, many teachers will say that they like all their students but, on close reflection, are able to notice differences in their responses. These differences can help us detect whether a young person is managing to elicit positive feelings from others, which can have a large impact on the self-esteem building climate in which they live.

The Indicator takes about 10 minutes to complete and score using this method.

2. Completed by an adult and student working together

This is the best way if the development work is likely to be done on a one-to-one basis or small group basis. When the assessment is completed in this way the interaction between the teaching professional and the young person as they do this task will set the tone for their future work together.

This method can take up to one session, or even more if the teaching professional decides to use it to get to know the student better.

Completing the Self-Esteem Indicator

Photocopy the Indicator given on page 135 of this manual and fill in the name, class and age of the student, plus the name of the assessor and the date.

Go through the Indicator question by question and rate each of the 30 items in turn by circling your chosen rating.

Rate each item on a four-point scale (ranging from 0–3). The choices are:

3 = 'most of the time'
2 = 'quite often'
1 = 'occasionally'
0 = 'almost never'

The ratings are then added up to produce an overall self-esteem score and three components scores, following the procedure below.

The completed record sheet should be kept with the student's records so that comparisons can be made later when the assessment is re-applied once some development work has taken place.

Scoring the Self-Esteem Indicator

Once the items have been read and rated, the ratings that have been circled are totalled to provide the student's **overall self-esteem score** (the higher the score, the higher the level of self-esteem).

Then consult the Interpretation Guide on page 21 to interpret the overall self-esteem score, which will fall into one of four categories – very low, vulnerable, good or high.

Next, follow the instructions on the Scoring Overlay provided at the back of this manual to obtain the **three component scores**, each of which relates to one of the three main components of self-esteem:

sense of self

sense of belonging

sense of personal power.

Then look at these component scores that reflect each of the three main components of self-esteem. These clearly show which is the strongest and which is the weakest component of the student's self-esteem. At this point the relative position of the scores to one another is what is important, not the scores themselves. At this level of interpretation the professional needs to see which component of self-esteem is stronger in relation to the others and which weaker. If a student has a low overall self-esteem score, his or her component scores are likely to be low on all components. However, the differences between them will be helpful when designing a self-esteem building programme. For example, if a particular young person's sense of self is stronger than his or her sense of belonging (even though both are low), it shows that the individual's awareness of self can provide an area where positives and encouragement can be easily given while the harder work of building the sense of belonging is carried out. Giving this young person a sense of accomplishment in one area will put him or her in a more receptive state for managing harder challenges such as taking risks and starting to make stronger peer relationships.

Interpretation Guide

Overall self-esteem score

The more 'most of the time' or 'quite often' ratings you gave, the higher the overall self-esteem score will be. Conversely, the more questions you rated as 'occasionally' or 'almost never', the lower this figure will be.

The chart below shows the different levels of self-esteem in relation to the overall self-esteem score, and the level of intervention required.

Overall self-esteem score	Level	Description	Level of intervention
69–90	High	Confident and at ease with self, other people and the world most of the time. Any knocks are quickly recovered from.	Maintenance.
46–68	Good	Feels good about self, but takes knocks now and again. Can take a bit of time to build back up again.	Maintenance and specific self-esteem building when knocked.
23–45	Vulnerable	Tends not to feel very confident and many incidents make the student feel worse about self. Emotionally quite fragile. Hard to build confidence up.	Self-esteem building on a day-to-day basis in classroom and through some form of extra support such as peer mentors, classroom assistance, after-school clubs.
0–22	Very low	Depressed or very challenging behaviour to cover this up. Needs support, encouragement and people with a strong belief in the student to change this behaviour/level of self-esteem.	Repair needed. Intensive, specific help from significant adults with whom the student has a good relationship.

This score will give you your first level of information for your 'diagnosis'. These scores tend to confirm a teaching professional's intuitive sense of a student's self-esteem. The suggestions on the grid concerning 'level of intervention' indicate the level of intensity and focus a student is likely to need in future self-esteem development work.

Component scores

Compare the component scores to find out which of the three main components is highest and which is lowest. **This is important information as it helps you identify where the main problem lies and where there is some basic strength from which you can build.** The definition of each of the component scores is given next.

Sense of self

Sense of self refers to the extent to which the young people know themselves well and are comfortable with who they are and what they are like. When it is high they believe they are valuable because they are themselves and unique. They are beginning to have a sense that no-one else can bring to the world the special qualities that are theirs. They know themselves reasonably well and are comfortable with their emotional states, which they will be learning how to handle.

Note: Children only begin to be able to use their own internal resources to manage all their emotional states successfully from around the age of eight upwards. After this, they can assess the situation, conceptualise a variety of responses and have more success in using solitary strategies such as using positive self-talk.

Sense of belonging

Sense of belonging refers to the extent to which young people feel as if they are part of a social group and find a sense of security and pride through that. Human beings are social creatures and we may prefer to be with one good friend, a few good friends or a number of large groups but, whatever our personal friendship patterns, we still need to feel as if we 'belong' somewhere. To belong, young people need reasonable friendship skills and the capacity to connect.

Note: Social skills and sharing will be harder to develop for individuals who are insecure. This insecurity may well last through the primary years and into the secondary years. The period of transition from elementary to secondary education can be particularly traumatising for young people. If they were insecure as young children, this problem is likely to reoccur at that point and limit their social skills again.

Sense of personal power

Sense of personal power refers to the extent to which young people have a sense of their own capability and forcefulness. They are starting to believe that they can have an impact on other people and the world and are able to learn new skills. They have a sense that their thoughts, feelings and opinions matter. This component of self-esteem is the greatest predictor of success in later life.

Note: The beginnings of personal power start when a child can crawl – an action that they can initiate as well as choosing the direction in which they will move. They are then no longer at the mercy of another person's wishes about their position. This is reinforced when they begin to walk and strengthened even further when their fine motor co-ordination reaches the point when they can pick up small objects, move them and choose which objects they want. It is the basis of adult independence and, by the time they get to school, patterns of personal power will be quite well established since it began to develop so early in their lives. Students who have learned a helpless and aggressive or passive approach early in life will need specific help by the time they are in their teens to unlearn old responses and relearn new, more powerful ones.

Using the scores in your work

Working with young people with low self-esteem

Low self-esteem is an accompanying factor to both poor academic performance and challenging behaviour. So students with whom you may work to develop self-esteem will frequently have low academic scores or be displaying challenging behaviour. As seen from the trial data (see Chapter 3), changes in these aspects were evident once the students had been assessed and given a period of time during which they experienced various self-esteem raising activities in the assertiveness training programme.

We can consider three categories of students when planning self-esteem development:

- self-esteem *maintenance only*;
- self-esteem *building*;
- self-esteem *repair*.

In each of these categories, the Self-Esteem Indicator provides valuable insight into the areas that need the most help, as well as the type of help that will work best.

The young people in the 'maintenance' category need far less intensive development activity than the ones in the 'repair' category. The students in the self-esteem 'building' category require a medium amount of focus and energy.

The distinctions between the categories can also be seen in the Interpretation Guide for the overall self-esteem score on page 21. Young people with high or good self-esteem scores will need to be learning in an esteeming culture with a good proportion of praise for doing well, appreciation for being a unique being, and constructive negative feedback so that they will know how to rectify a mistake. This will maintain their self-esteem quite adequately. Occasionally students who have good self-esteem may need a short extra focus to help them build their self-esteem again if they have dipped in response to some life event, such as parental separation or the birth of a new sibling.

Young people with vulnerable self-esteem are likely to need a focused self-esteem building programme. This can take place in the class, in one-to-one sessions or in small groups. One or more of their main components of self-esteem will be low and will need to be reinforced and re-built. The more they are in an esteeming environment, the better they will respond to any extra self-esteem building programme.

Finally, young people with very low self-esteem need a 'repair' programme, which will work more deeply than the self-esteem building programmes mentioned above. It is likely that the repair work will also need to involve some sort of therapeutic element, such as counselling. The students' sense of alienation will be very strong in this case, and they will find it hard to find something to value in themselves unless that belief is provided by an adult or peer they can come to respect.

Young people with a variety of special educational needs

One way of categorising students who need help with self-esteem development is to consider those with special educational needs as a discrete group. These young people frequently have a poor self-image and lack of self-worth, which is shown on the Self-Esteem Indicator by a 'very low' or 'vulnerable' overall self-esteem score.

These students, like many of us, tend to compare themselves with others. Doing this frequently and believing themselves to come out poorly in the comparison to their peers can lead to any or all of the self-esteem components being badly affected. The more badly affected these are, the more the students then fall back on inappropriate behaviour in an attempt to express their complicated feelings in response to what they experience. The behaviour will escalate if nothing is done to address it.

Self-esteem assessment and a focused group programme that gives sensitive and yet unobtrusive support to these young people is very helpful in building a sense of belonging and sense of self. As these two components develop they can form a solid foundation for the young people from which they can deal more effectively with feelings such as frustration and embarrassment. Managing these complicated and difficult emotions better will positively influence their sense of personal power.

Raising self-esteem in secondary schools

The task of developing self-esteem in teenagers is far more challenging than doing this work with younger children. During her research, the author and her associates discovered that it was far more effective in secondary schools to carry out this development work through delivering skills training programmes than by using brief activities related to the three components of self-esteem as part of the daily lessons.

There are several reasons for this, some concerning the nature of young people and their particular needs and others concerning the nature of the secondary school system.

To have an impact on the self-esteem of young people of this age group you need:

- a good relationship with the group or individual;
- time (preferably two terms, but a minimum of one);
- a skills focus that they can relate to their everyday lives.

A good relationship

Secondary schools focus strongly on knowledge and achievements as a preparation for adult life. Owing to this, students move from one teacher to another, thus making the special relationship with a supportive adult hard to develop. For people of any age to change their attitudes and behaviour successfully, the presence of an encouraging person whom they trust and respect will make a significant difference. This is certainly true of teenagers who are so busy trying to work out who they are and how they should respond to things that they adopt masks and styles to conceal their vulnerability, making it hard for them to learn and try new things unless they are in the right environment.

Time

Research on behavioural change in group work has demonstrated that, for a successful change in attitudes and behaviour that can be generalised outside the supporting group, two terms of support is optimal. A shorter duration can result in the new behaviour not lasting or never really being transferred outside the group. This is because the social and emotional habits young people have developed are quite entrenched by this stage – short activities as part of a wider lesson will not impinge greatly on their consciousness, and certainly not on their self-concept. However, most young people who took part in a focused programme during this research showed that they had grasped the basics of a different attitude and knew how to use the skills after one term (*unpublished research*, Professor Paul Cooper, Nurture Group Conference, May 2002).

Skills focus

By the teenage years young people are used to being consumers, are able to be sophisticated and discriminating, and may be motivated by something that can answer the question: 'What's in it for me?'. If knowledge or learning is presented in a way that hooks into that question, young people are more likely to respond. Thus the more relevance they can see in the learning experience to problems they encounter in their everyday lives, the more motivated they will be and, therefore, the more likely to want to change.

The best way to raise self-esteem in secondary schools is undoubtedly to have a whole school self-esteem policy, as described on pages 27 and 43. In this case many members of staff will have had special training in self-esteem building and everyone will be aware of the actions and attitudes that make a real difference. In practice, few secondary schools focus on self-esteem raising, although it is frequently acknowledged as an important aspect to be addressed through the teaching and pastoral systems.

Self-esteem development can be achieved via several routes within a school. One is through PSHE sessions with a focus on personal and social learning. Secondly, it can be done as part of the pastoral provision for students who are experiencing some difficulties behaviourally, emotionally or with their learning.

Social skills training is an effective way to address self-esteem building. The combination of acquiring personally relevant skills and doing this within an environment that is safe, respectful and supportive works well. Personal and social skills such as assertiveness, friendship-making, conflict resolution, anger management, mood control, problem-solving and goal-setting are particularly helpful. Examples of a selection of these are given in the 'Activities and example programmes' section of this manual, page 41. In addition to developing general self-esteem, judicious selection of the *type* of skills programme used can help to develop each of the different components of self-esteem. For example, a programme on assertiveness is particularly effective in developing a sense of personal power, one on friendship-making supports a sense of belonging and one on goal-setting is excellent for developing a stronger sense of self.

DESIGNING AND IMPLEMENTING
A SELF-ESTEEM BUILDING PROGRAMME

There are different ways to tackle a self-esteem issue in a school, from a full-blown whole school initiative to a small programme for one individual. If using a whole school approach, the professionals working with the students need to carry out a series of assessments within the school using the Self-Esteem Indicator. A random selection can be made to gauge the overall self-esteem levels in the school. Alternatively, specific individuals or groups can be selected if they are suspected of having vulnerable self-esteem.

Whole setting approach

If the level of self-esteem is found to be generally 'good' (that is, an average overall self-esteem score of 46 or more) when the Self-Esteem Indicator scores are collated in a school, conducting an audit of the following current school practices is useful:

- current pastoral activities
- the use of active listening
- positive and negative feedback
- positive behaviour management
- use of different teaching styles
- awareness of different learning styles
- use of 'multiple intelligence' practices
- school council
- peer mentors
- anti-bullying policies
- behaviour policy.

This review would give some guidance as to what is working well and what could be added or improved upon to make the environment even more positively self-esteem building. The creation of this type of warm and supportive, yet challenging, environment is one of the best ways to improve the security, self-perception and personal capabilities of both the staff and the students. Changes in behaviour and performance will be accelerated with this type of support to complement the other teaching methods.

Small groups

Where assessments have been done with small groups of students who are suspected of having low self-esteem, the next step is to begin designing the right development programme for that group according to the areas of vulnerability highlighted by the Indicator. The high and low scores on the main components of self-esteem will guide this and a checklist of factors that increase the success of these programmes is given later in this chapter on page 31. Examples of programmes can be found in the section entitled 'Activities and sample programmes' on page 41. Consciously doing activities such as Activity 1 'Active listening' and Activity 3 'Positive praise' on a regular basis with these students will also help to create an atmosphere in which self-esteem can be built more easily.

Individuals

Sometimes one student stands out as being particularly distressed, disturbed or distracted in their behaviour. Alternatively, they may have shown themselves to be more responsive to one-to-one attention than when they are just one in a group of other students. If this is the case, an option is to assess them individually, and then develop an intervention for them alone. The Indicator will show their overall level of self-esteem and the area on which to concentrate, and this is the best way to start preparing a specific and focused intervention for them. These interventions can range from a little extra focused attention within the classroom to referring them to the learning support unit and school counsellor or a peer mentor. The level of their overall self-esteem, the component of self-esteem that is most vulnerable and their past history will help to dictate the best approach.

Thus, we can see that there are various options to choose from when considering what to do about raising self-esteem in young people. One of the constraints that schools often face is a lack of resources to tackle the problem. Time, energy and money are necessary to make any of these initiatives work, but particularly time. These self-esteem building programmes and the self-esteem building environment take time to develop and to begin to operate successfully. Nevertheless, the students *do* respond well to these interventions and, in particular, to an accumulation of small, everyday actions such as praise, well-phrased negative feedback and plenty of smiles.

Students who have severe social and emotional difficulties

Students who have severe social and emotional difficulties, and who have responded to their circumstances by being very disruptive and oppositional, initially get worse when they are met by this self-esteem building approach. Their challenging behaviour and negative self-esteem are likely to escalate since this attempt to reflect back to them a positive picture of themselves will be a strong challenge to their own internal negative self-image. Once this has happened they will have to try to return to a more familiar internal position again. These students will strongly oppose this attempt to change their view of themselves but, even more importantly, they will be suspicious of this approach. Aggression is the most likely behavioural option for them as they try to cover their unease and any fear they may feel. Also they are unlikely to trust adults in general, so only time and experiencing a slow build-up of trust are likely to change their minds.

Although it may sound counter-intuitive and difficult to do when you are hoping to change things for the better, it is important to initially limit the number of positive and appreciative comments you make with young people such as these. Having been used to a steady diet of negatives (from themselves and many other people) for a long time, a sudden change to all positives is too much for them to accept. Instead, a step-by-step approach is needed, only introducing positive feedback gradually. For example, it is advisable to start by giving these students more negative than positive feedback about their work or behaviour – as this pattern is more like the communication pattern they are used to, they will be more prepared to accept this without fighting you and it does not pose too great a challenge to their own self-image yet. Gradually the proportion of negatives to positives for students with exceptionally challenging behaviour can be shifted until many more positive than negative statements are made. Students who have not suffered such damage to their trust and their social and emotional development can start with the positive reinforcement pattern of more positives than negatives without needing this step-by-step approach. (Our research in November 2001 strongly showed this step-by-step approach to be appropriate when feedback was given in varying proportions to different groups of students.)

Creating an esteeming environment

As we have seen, self-esteem is a changeable phenomenon. For instance, if a student moves from one school to another, or even from one subject teacher to another, their sense of belonging may dip for a while as they adjust and find themselves a role and place in the new situation. How successful they are in recovering from this will depend greatly on how well they have managed in the past and how well they are supported in the new environment. Given this sensitivity to outside circumstances, it is extremely important to create an environment in a school, classroom, group or behaviour support unit that provides the basic conditions within which self-esteem can flourish. Once this is in place, any specific self-esteem building programme that may be organised for vulnerable individuals will be particularly effective.

Factors that influence self-esteem

Three factors are important when planning the creation of the self-esteem enhancing environment needed by the students. These factors are discussed in turn below.

1. Your input

The input of significant adults affects young people very strongly, often much more than the adults imagine. As the early research by Coopersmith (1967) showed, children need adults to care for them and to express this in recognisable and respectful ways. This is easy to say but much harder to do in a busy educational environment with academic standards to be achieved. However, without this students are more likely to push boundaries, escalate their attention-seeking behaviour and find less than desirable ways to assert their individuality and needs – all of which will be detrimental to their academic success.

Teachers or carers who are involved, warm and accepting of the students (though not necessarily of their behaviour), have realistic expectations, demonstrate consistency about boundaries and model the kind of attitudes and behaviour they want to see in the young people will create a rich environment for the growth of all the components of self-esteem. This input is particularly relevant for building a sense of self and a sense of personal power.

2. The social value of the class

Young people place different values on belonging to different groups. Sometimes these are internally generated values (for example, some gangs or sports teams seem to convey particular status) and sometimes the value is a reflection of a wider culture (for example, respect for members of the senior year in a secondary school reflects the cultural value given to 'being grown up'). A sense of belonging being gained by association with the most socially desirable groups is more obvious in secondary schools. Teachers can increase the social value of their classes by valuing good results and sports achievements, but also by overtly recognising and publicly praising social and emotional achievements such as kindness to others, a no-blame response and honest communication. This factor plays an important part in the development of a sense of belonging.

3. The teaching approach

This tends to reinforce the impact of the input from the adults (factor 1), since it involves giving positive feedback, using natural learning opportunities when they occur, providing assertiveness and problem-solving skills training, using different teaching styles to fit different learners and allowing a lot of time for practice. These are particularly powerful ways to develop personal power in the individual students.

Critical success factors in self-esteem building programmes

The factors that must be present in dedicated self-esteem building programmes are:

1. an atmosphere in which attitude changes can take place
2. opportunities for skills training and practice
3. opportunities for gaining personal and interpersonal knowledge
4. set objectives
5. an articulated theory of self-esteem
6. a systematic and cumulative programme
7. assessment
8. proficient facilitators.

Each of these is discussed separately below.

1. An atmosphere in which attitude changes can take place
This means that the environment should be:

- accepting – to encourage trust and risk-taking;
- challenging – to provide a stimulus for change;
- empathic – to support self-discovery.

2. Opportunities for skills training and practice
Each component has different skills attached to it and students need time and practice to gain mastery. The typical skills that need to be taught for each of the three components are as follows:

- **sense of self** – accurate self-description, identifying and expressing emotions;
- **sense of belonging** – friendship-making, communication, negotiation;
- **sense of personal power** – accurate self-appraisal, goal-setting, self-support techniques, decision-making.

3. Opportunities for gaining personal and interpersonal knowledge
Each component has different aspects of self-awareness to it and requires exercises to help the student focus on the appropriate level of awareness:

- **sense of self** – own behaviour and feeling patterns, own qualities;
- **sense of belonging** – information about other people and their thoughts, interests, feelings and behaviour;
- **sense of personal power** – past successes, inner strengths, external resources and support systems.

4. Set objectives

The programme needs to have some general objectives, such as:

- increasing awareness of the importance of self-esteem;
- finding new ways to deal with students' defensiveness and resistance to change;
- changing self-defeating behaviours and/or acquiring new skills;
- developing a sense of self, belonging and/or personal power.

The choice of any or all of these objectives helps to focus the content of the programme.

5. An articulated theory of self-esteem

A programme needs to be based on and consistent with a particular theory of self-esteem. For example, if your theory of self-esteem were that it is the product of the messages given to children from their social culture, as the social scientists believe, your programme would focus on this aspect alone. It would have activities and reflective sessions that helped the participants to become aware of the way their behaviour is shaped by the expectations significant people in their lives might have of them. It would not have activities that focused, for instance, on future aspirations and ways the individuals might reach their full potential (these would be present in a self-esteem building programme based on humanistic psychology theories).

Having a clear theory that guides the choice of the activities within a programme, when it is combined with the information gained from the Indicator, ensures cohesiveness of the activities and promotes a sense of belonging since it enhances security.

6. A systematic and cumulative programme

In point 5 above, the goal was to make the programme as cohesive as possible. The goal here is to make it developmentally integrated:

- each step has a goal;
- each step has clear activities designed to reach that goal;
- each step and its activities builds on the one before.

For example, in the case in point 5, the programme might begin with activities designed to help the students think about the different influential groups in their lives, such as parents, friends, teachers and family. The goal for this step would be to raise awareness about the number of groups a person is part of. The next step would be to examine the different messages that each group gives the individual, the goal here being to raise awareness about the content of the social messages received. The third step would be to help the students work out which messages they would like to hear more, perhaps through presenting alternatives and showing videos of different societies. The fourth step might be to set up a situation where the teacher and the students give one another some of their preferred messages during classroom time for a month. The goal for this step, for example, might be to acquire the skill of giving and receiving compliments.

This factor particularly supports both a sense of belonging and a sense of personal power.

7. Assessment

In the example above the students might have been assessed by using the Self-Esteem Indicator and observing classroom behaviour, academic achievements and peer relationships. Alternatively, they could assess themselves, perhaps by developing their own criteria. Assessing again within two weeks of the programme finishing and again some three to six months later will give a good picture of whether there have been any changes and whether they have lasted. This will enhance the senses of self and personal power since it will focus the individuals on themselves and on what they can achieve by applying focused effort.

8. Proficient facilitators

The skills required by the professionals implementing a focused self-esteem building programme are varied. For example, they need to be able to teach, coach, champion, listen well, challenge respectfully and firmly, and be flexible. The programme as a whole needs to be more active than a process such as counselling (although counselling may form a part of it), yet more person-centred and individualised than traditional teaching. Facilitators also need to be able to generate a climate of trust through their warmth and acceptance. A facilitator who can do this will weave together support for the three components of self-esteem through both the content *and* the process of the programme.

See Section 6 in the section entitled 'Activities and example programmes' on page 41 for an example of the planning and designing of a general self-esteem building programme.

CASE STUDIES

The case studies in this chapter illustrate how the Self-Esteem Indicator helped three students develop much stronger self-esteem.

Case study 1: A low sense of self

In common with many girls in her year group, Hayley was keen on the latest fashion and boys. She had no interest in her schoolwork and spent much of her time worrying about her weight and how she looked. She was referred to the behaviour support unit because her behaviour in the classrooms had become almost impossible to manage. Hayley frequently left the school grounds (being absent for at least part of the day), refused to do her homework, and acted aggressively to any teacher who questioned her about this.

The support unit manager to whom Hayley was assigned completed the Self-Esteem Indicator and saw that, while Hayley's sense of personal power was high in relation to her other scores, her sense of self was very low. This is a typical pattern for students with severe or moderate learning difficulties who often have many emotional problems too, and these compound their learning difficulties.

Overall self-esteem score		40
Sense of self component score		8
Sense of belonging component score		14
Sense of personal power component score		18

With such high personal power scores, the manager knew that it was important not to enter into a power battle with the girl. Hayley needed to feel that she was in control and was needed to provide help to others rather than receiving help herself. The manager therefore suggested that Hayley could help her set up a programme with the other girls in the unit, to focus on the theme of 'looking good on the outside and feeling good on the inside'. Her interest in and awareness of fashion was the key to recruiting her for the programme. In fact, all the girls had been asked to help design and deliver the programme, as each could contribute to the others' learning.

Hayley's sense of self began to emerge during the programme as she worked through the self-awareness exercises with her peers. They worked with art, drama and music, experimenting to find out what they enjoyed and what made them feel and look good. The use of mirrors, clothes, props and film made it a memorable journey for all of them. Hayley discovered that she enjoyed singing and that she had a strong voice that sounded similar to one of her pop idols. Although still needing to find some identity by allying herself with a public figure, she did learn more about herself as a unique individual and, during the course of the programme, improved her behaviour in the classrooms and played truant far less often.

Case study 2: A low sense of belonging

George was 15 years old, had been in the school for two years, and had still not made any good friends. He had learning difficulties and very little belief in himself; his home life was fairly chaotic as his stepfather worked away during the week, his mother worked shifts at a local hospital and his stepsisters appeared to dominate the household because they were older than him. George's teachers had noticed that he could be aggressive towards some of the other students in the class, particularly the girls. Sometimes he seemed to desperately want to form friendships, but his year tutor felt that George did not possess good friendship-making skills. Thus, while he often started well, his behaviour would begin to deteriorate and the other students would get fed up with him or try to avoid him. Nothing seemed to be making a difference to his behaviour and, if anything, it was getting worse as he went through the year.

The tutor decided to use the Self-Esteem Indicator to help her identify the most problematic component of George's self-esteem. His overall self-esteem score was near the top of the very low range. However, when the component scores were calculated, it was clear that his sense of belonging was very low compared to the other two components.

Overall self-esteem score	20
Sense of self component score	10
Sense of belonging component score	4
Sense of personal power component score	6

George was already assigned to the learning support unit for several periods during the week, so he was invited to join three other students there every morning in order to prepare themselves positively for the learning they would encounter that day. Two of the other students in the group were far more socially skilled than George, and soon the small group found that they had plenty to say to one another each morning.

To help settle George into the group over the next few weeks, the learning support tutor made sure that the lessons included more pairs work and group discussion than before. His behaviour tended to be most aggressive before breaks when he was about to confront the difficulty of not having a core of friends at breaktimes. He began to come back to the unit at these times to help the tutor with various tasks. Gradually he began to talk to the others from his morning group when they were *outside* the unit and from that point on he started to gain some confidence about having 'friendship-making' skills. The small group continued to support each other outside as well as inside the unit and was very pro-active about helping new students once they had been referred to the learning support unit. This too seemed to help George believe that he was likeable. After two terms of support he had managed to form a wider group of friends with whom he played football.

Case study 3: A low sense of personal power

Nathan, a 14-year-old boy in a city school, was referred to the learning support unit. He had been falling behind in all his subjects and was starting to be fairly disruptive in the classrooms, making angry and sarcastic comments in a low voice throughout the lessons. He said he was bored and that the teachers didn't understand him. Compared to earlier years when he had seemed to enjoy new challenges, Nathan now believed that he couldn't tackle new topics or concepts and would give up easily. He now obviously had little self-belief and reinforced this with a continual stream of negative messages to himself, such as 'I'm too stupid to do that' and 'I know I can't do that, it's too hard'.

The head of the support unit used the Self-Esteem Indicator to investigate what help Nathan needed most, and soon discovered that he scored lowest on personal power, with an overall self-esteem score in the vulnerable range.

Overall self-esteem score	32
Sense of self component score	10
Sense of belonging component score	18
Sense of personal power component score	4

She subsequently found out through the head of year that Nathan was living with his grandparents while his parents worked abroad. His grandparents were concerned about him but felt unable to help him as he spent much of his leisure time with his girlfriend so they seldom saw him. He seemed to be very dependent on his girlfriend and did not relate much to other people. On reflection, his grandparents thought that this had happened about the time his parents had gone abroad and recalled that he had had a similar reaction some years before when his parents had worked abroad for a previous short spell.

Nathan was given several options for development work and was asked for his preference. He chose to work with the learning mentor rather than join a social skills group or have extra curriculum tutoring. He knew the mentor a little and seemed to get on quite well with him.

Nathan learnt various self-help strategies while working with the learning mentor. He began to use more positive 'self-talk', which automatically reduced the number of negative messages he gave himself during the day. Having a good relationship with an adult who encouraged and praised him worked well for Nathan, and he quickly began to act more self-confidently in regard to his work. They realised that there were a couple of areas where he had not properly understood the basics of a subject and Nathan then began to have extra support to catch up. As long as he could also have contact with the learning mentor he was happy to have contact with the subject tutor. Over a term he began to socialise more with some other students in his year group and seemed to settle down better with his grandparents. Although still not achieving his full potential, Nathan's work improved measurably and his self-belief strengthened considerably.

BIBLIOGRAPHY

BOND, T. (1990) *Games for Social and Life Skills*. Cheltenham: Stanley Thornes.

BORBA, M. (1994) *Esteem Builder's Resources*. California: Jalmer Press.

BORBA, M. and BORBA, C. (1978) *Self-Esteem: A Classroom Affair*. San Francisco: HarperSanFrancisco.

BRANDEN, N. (1969) *The Psychology of Self-Esteem*. London: Bantam.

CANFIELD, J. AND WELLS, H. (1994) *101 Ways to Enhance Self-Concept in the Classroom*. Hemel Hempstead: Allyn and Bacon.

COOPERSMITH, S. (1967) *The Antecedents of Self-Esteem*. Oxford: W.H. Freeman and Company.

DAMASCIO, A. (1994) *Descartes' Error: Emotion, Reason and the Human Brain*. New York: GP Puttnam's & Sons.

GILBERT, I. (2002) *Essential Motivation in the Classroom*. London: Routledge Falmer.

GOTTMAN, J. (1997) *The Heart of Parenting*. London: Bloomsbury Publishing.

HERTFORDSHIRE COUNTY COUNCIL. (1998) *A Handbook containing a Framework for the Assessment of Personal and Social Development*. Hertfordshire Education Services.

HUMPHREYS, T. (1993) *Self-Esteem: The Key to Your Child's Education*. Dublin: Gill and Macmillan Ltd (New Leaf).

ILLSLEY CLARKE, J. (1978) *Self-Esteem: A Family Affair*. New York: Harper and Row Publishers.

ILLSLEY CLARKE, J. (1981) *Self-Esteem: A Family Affair – Leader Guide*. New York: Harper and Row Publishers.

KATZ, A. (1999) *Leading Lads Report*, based on Tomorrow's Men Survey, sponsored by Topman. East Moseley, Surrey: Young Voice.

LAWRENCE, D. (1996) *Enhancing Self-Esteem in the Classroom – Second Edition.* London: Paul Chapman Publishing Ltd.

MEHRABIAN, A. (1976) *Silent Messages.* Andover: Wadsworth Publishing.

MORRIS, E. (1997) *Building Self-Esteem in Children, Workbook.* Gloucester: Buckholdt Publishing.

MORRIS, E. (2002) *An Emotionally Literate Approach to Assertiveness Training.* Milton Keynes: Incentive Publishing.

MRUK, C.J. (1999) *Self-Esteem: Research, Theory and Practice – Second Edition.* London: Springer Publishing Company.

ROBERTS, R. (1995) *Self-Esteem and Successful Early Learning.* London: Hodder and Stoughton Educational.

ROSENBERG, M. (1965) *Society and the Adolescent Self-Image.* USA: Princeton University Press.

SALOVEY, P. AND MEYER, J. (1990) Emotional intelligence. *Imagination, Cognition and Personality*, **9**.

Self-Esteem Advisory Service www.selfesteemadvisoryservice.org

SHARP, P. (2001) *Nurturing Emotional Literacy.* London: David Fulton Publishers.

YOUNGS, B. (1992) *Enhancing the Educator's Self-Esteem: It's Your Criteria – Number 1.* California: Jalmer Press.

ZACK, L. (1995) *Building Self-Esteem through the Museum of the Self.* Minnesota: Free Spirit Publishing Inc.

ACTIVITIES AND
EXAMPLE PROGRAMMES

INTRODUCTION TO THE OPTIONS AVAILABLE

Using the activities and programmes

This section contains a selection of activities and programme outlines that can be used as part of your school's self-esteem building initiative. During the research and trialling of the Self-Esteem Indicator, it was found to be far more effective in secondary schools to carry out development work on self-esteem through delivering skills training programmes rather than by using brief activities related to the three components of self-esteem as part of the daily lessons. (Activities were found to work well with younger children, and are used in *Insight Pre-School* and *Insight Primary*, the two other manuals in the *Insight Series*.) The reasons for this have been elaborated on pages 24 to 26.

The user therefore has various options. Owing to the structure of secondary school education, it is most practical either to have a whole school self-esteem building policy or to provide specific self-esteem building programmes. Even if the former option is taken, specific programmes can also be used.

Option 1: A whole school self-esteem policy

Although a whole school self-esteem policy does not target particular individuals or specific weak components of self-esteem, it does support every person within the school. If all the staff are in favour of it, it can also be extremely effective in changing the culture in a school. A whole school policy can be rendered even more effective by taking sample assessments from different year groups to ascertain whether particular components of self-esteem are lower than others. In the event that one component is weaker than the others throughout the whole school, or one component is weaker in certain year groups, steps can be taken to address this by using some of the suggestions below, such as providing the year groups with specific programmes or a particular personal focus during their PSHE sessions during the year.

Suggestions from **Section 1 'Creating a self-esteem building environment'**, pages 47 to 50, are particularly useful in this instance. This section provides a range of activities or processes that can be put in place to enhance the self-esteem of everyone in the school, from students to support staff.

Option 2: Cascading of self-esteem building skills

A further option is to train as many staff members as possible in self-esteem building techniques so that these are used on a daily basis in as many classes as possible. This is a step down from a whole school policy, but is extremely helpful in maintaining and supporting the self-esteem levels of the majority of the students.

In the research we have conducted throughout all the schools, the teaching professionals who had had basic training in self-esteem building made the biggest impact on their students' self-esteem, irrespective of the type of intervention used.

The activities found in **Section 2 'Supporting professionals'**, on pages 51 to 53, will be useful for this option. One of the easiest ways to help students develop their self-esteem is for the adults working with them to have sound self-esteem too. This section, therefore, provides a variety of tips and pointers to help teaching professionals keep their own self-esteem topped up, or to help them build it if it is lower than they would like it to be. Training in self-esteem building techniques for use in the classroom is also available through nferNelson.

Option 3: Specific self-esteem building programmes

This option is less complex, but also less effective when there is a wide variety of people requiring self-esteem building support in the school system. It involves selecting groups of students to receive particular programmes for self-esteem building. These groups can be year groups, tutor groups and informal groups of individuals referred to the learning support unit, or any other group that might be identified as having difficulties in some areas. These students can receive a programme, such as social skills training, self-esteem building or assertiveness training, in periods set aside for PSHE or in the time in which they are allocated a support teacher. For example, some schools have done this in lunch periods for students who have had difficulty managing their free time successfully. **Sections 3 to 6**, which contain various **skills training programmes**, are presented on pages 55 to 114 and can make a great contribution to this option.

Introduction to the programmes

As explained on pages 24 and 43, skills-based programmes delivered over a period of time have been found to be a more effective way than brief activities to address self-esteem building with this age group. The combination of acquiring personally relevant skills and doing this within an environment that is safe, respectful and supportive works well. Personal and social skills such as assertiveness, friendship-making, conflict resolution, anger management, mood control, problem-solving and goal-setting are particularly helpful, and so examples of a selection of these are presented here. In addition to developing general self-esteem, judicious selection of the *type* of skills programme used can help to develop each of the different components of self-esteem. For example, a programme on assertiveness is particularly effective in developing a sense of personal power, one on friendship-making supports a sense of belonging and one on goal-setting is excellent for developing a stronger sense of self. These courses work particularly well with young people when they are used in conjunction with the types of self-esteem building approaches found in Options 1 and 2.

You can choose *any* programme that has the features described in the 'critical factors checklist' on page 31. However, examples of specific programmes are provided in this section to illustrate how such programmes can raise self-esteem generally as well as impact on the three separate components of self-esteem. The sample programmes suggested for each component are very different in style and length as these are the formats that fit their particular content and purpose – the important thing is that each has the main objective of developing self-esteem. Therefore, any programme you choose to implement, whether it be one of those suggested here or one you select from elsewhere, needs to have this clear objective plus a flexible structure to accommodate the students' individual learning needs and to facilitate student discussion. The research found an assertiveness programme to be particularly valuable in raising overall self-esteem through increasing all of the three main components, so it has been reproduced here in its entirety. The other two programmes can also be expanded or adapted to suit your school's needs.

One of the most significant elements of success for these programmes is the creation of the right psychological or emotional environment for learning. For example, a group where the students have a learning experience that accepts their differences and respects their contributions and honest communications will obtain different results to a group where they are only taught skills and are not encouraged to participate democratically. The feedback from students who have participated in these programmes has all emphasised their appreciation of the opportunity to learn with and from one another and to feel valued.

Some tips for running these programmes have been gleaned from the feedback received from students:

- Have fun.
- Establish ground rules.
- Listen without judging.
- Be democratic.
- Practise what you preach, especially during the sessions.
- Make the room as user-friendly as possible, for example, make sure there are no interruptions, that people can see, and that water is provided.

CREATING A SELF-ESTEEM BUILDING ENVIRONMENT

Activity 1: Active listening

Learn how to listen carefully. Listening carefully is a gift you can give to everyone as it conveys interest, respect and empathy. There are many levels to the words students say to you. Emotions, hidden agendas, developing values, hesitation, uncertainty and bravado are all there in the words and the way they are said. Learning to listen to, pick up on and respond to the different levels gives you more information about the students and builds a more successful learning relationship.

Activity 2: Make learning enjoyable

Make learning as enjoyable as possible for both you and the students. It is no great surprise that young people – and adults – learn well through having fun. Making games, quizzes, playlets, contests, etc. out of the material that needs to be learnt can make a difference to how well it is absorbed by the students. They use more of themselves as they get involved and their brains receive the information through multiple channels rather than only through their eyes and ears. They start to link learning with the emotion of pleasure or fun, and that emotional association helps them both recall and retain information and to feel good about learning.

Activity 3: Positive praise

Try to give each student you teach a particular piece of positive praise every week or at least every two weeks. Take a moment to work out what you have really appreciated about each student. Then tell them!

Activity 4: Little things mean alot

Little things – like a smile at a gloomy moment – can make a big impact. Small everyday things count as much as the big moments when a great achievement is made and celebrated. In fact the small everyday things are even more important because they are always available to support and acknowledge people, no matter how they feel about themselves. How often do you smile, give a word of encouragement or greet everyone as they come in?

Activity 5: Create an open environment

Create an open, caring environment. This can be achieved by listening well, being open to discussion, valuing ideas, feelings and thoughts from everyone and making sure that all the students are able (if not always willing!) to listen carefully to one another as well.

Activity 6: Be open-minded

Keep an open-minded, non-judgemental attitude. Being open and unbiased in your reactions to what the students – and your colleagues – say and think helps them feel safe to express themselves. As soon as people think they are going to be judged or criticised they tend to close up, refusing to talk about more sensitive subjects in order to protect themselves. This won't help them build their self-esteem, because they will be too scared to talk about what matters to them and get support in the areas of need.

Activity 7: Be patient

Change takes time, so be patient. You may think you have made yourself clear and asked students to do something differently but, rather than getting annoyed when they don't immediately start to change their behaviour, remember you will probably need to ask 20 times before the behaviour change starts happening. Yes, 20! This is how long it takes for a message about new behaviour to sink in and start becoming a habit. You can see why change takes time.

Activity 8: Discussion Time

Run Discussion Time (or Circle Time) regularly in your class. This is a period where students have more control to talk about things that they enjoy, to discuss what they think about various learning topics, and to relate their learning to events that happen to them throughout the day. This all helps them learn personal and social skills and attitudes in an easy way.

Activity 9: Walk in the student's shoes

Empathise by 'walking a mile in your student's shoes'. Stretch yourself every now and again to imagine as vividly as possible what it would be like to be a certain young person. To be that size, with that family, with that appearance – now what do you feel like and how would you behave? Empathy, the result of being able to actively listen, is a crucial ability for all adults working with children and young people.

Activity 10: Share

Tell the students a little about you and your 'journey' to becoming a teacher or something about the kinds of things you enjoy. Our research has shown us that young people respond well to hearing some of the 'life stories' of their teachers. The stories seem to provide models for the students, especially if the life story has been varied.

Activity 11: Thank people for 'being them'

Write your tutor group or classes a letter at the end of the year thanking them for 'being them'. Copy the letter for everybody, with a personal signature on each. Include a general appreciation, an illustration of a fun time you enjoyed with the students this year and a summary of all the positive things you have achieved together, and finish with good wishes for their future. At the end of the year teachers write reports and appraisals, but how many write to say thank you? If you haven't done this in the past, try it next time and see how you feel to write such a letter and how the students feel to have that kind of acknowledgement.

Activity 12: Guided visualisations

Use guided visualisations and stories to put across important life lessons. Young people often don't respond well to being confronted with a demand to think about themselves and their situation. Instead, they work better by hearing stories about other people who have managed in similar life situations in creative ways. Inviting guests to the school to talk to the students about their successes and failures as they tried to deal with difficulties in their lives can have even greater impact.

Activity 13: Emotional coaching

Learn how to be an 'emotional coach'. Like active listening, on which this process is based, this skill really helps students learn how to manage their emotions and deepens their self-control. It cannot be used often because it is quite time-consuming. However, used whenever possible, it provides a very good emotional training and support for students. It involves moving through five steps from becoming aware that a person is displaying some emotions, to active listening and naming the emotions that the person is experiencing, through to helping them work out how to manage themselves better in the situation (Gottman, 1997). Frequently, just doing some active listening with students is enough to help them calm down in awkward situations. In some cases, coaching them through new behaviours, such as making an apology or being assertive rather than aggressive, can be necessary.

Activity 14: The power of being a human being

Be aware that how you interact with anyone in the school at any time can build their self-esteem or undermine it. This is part of the power of being a human being! We matter to one another and another person's opinion of us can be a cause of happiness or hurt. If you are willing to take on the responsibility and the joy of making a difference all the time, this is the place to start.

Activity 15: Experiment

Think about what you are doing to encourage a certain type of behaviour. In a strange way we can invite a particular response from another person. For instance, if you talk pleasantly and co-operatively with people, they are more likely to be co-operative than if you habitually order them around. If you find that you are getting a particularly undesirable response from particular students on a regular basis, STOP and check what you yourself have just said or done that might have encouraged that kind of response. If you can, experiment by finding another way to respond and then see what reaction you get.

Activity 16: Let's have a debate

Hold class debates on themes such as co-operation versus competition, trust versus fear, openness versus deceit. People learn about themselves, relationships and the community when they can have debates about concrete examples of moral concepts. In schools there can be examples of petty thievery, bad feelings over losing a game, fear of bullies, etc. Use these examples for discussion in the class, and give the students an opportunity to work out ways to deal with the problems.

Activity 17: Play or pass

Let students 'pass' if they don't want to join in. It is important that people have the right to 'pass' if they don't want to contribute to that activity or discussion at a particular time. This engenders a feeling of security and personal power. If someone consistently 'passes', however, perhaps this is a signal that he or she has a bigger problem that requires private discussion. Alternatively, you could encourage the other students to talk about how they feel about that individual always passing so that the person will hear that he or she is important and cared about. This can often start a self-conscious individual on the road to joining in. Another option is to do more exercises in pairs for a while to build up friendships. After that friends can talk for one another in a larger group if they choose.

Activity 18: Who's who

Make a year group or tutor group 'Who's who'. This is like a directory they can dip into to find out more about each person in the group. Each person, including the teachers and support staff, can write a self-description to include their name, age, height, eye colour, special interests, friends' names, pets, great achievements, small successes, favourite foods, etc. You and the students can decide what information to include – Worksheet ☐1 provides a template for the directory if you wish to use it.

SUPPORTING PROFESSIONALS

Activity 19: You are unique

Know that *you* are unique and special too. In the intense activity of the classroom it is easy to forget about your own needs and to put yourself at the bottom of the list of things that need attention. Remind yourself that *you* count too, and organise some friends, colleagues or family to give you the positive reminders you need of your own uniqueness and importance.

Activity 20: Celebrate

Pat yourself on the back, congratulating yourself for all the things you accomplish. Things move so fast these days as more goals to achieve get crammed into the teaching time. It is easy to miss the successes – the smile from the young person who is usually unhappy, a poor reader suddenly improving, the project completed on time, the thanks from a worried parent. It is important to celebrate the little things and give yourself recognition for what you are achieving.

Activity 21: Accept praise

Ask a colleague to tell you the things about you that they enjoy. Make sure that you let the praise and appreciation in and don't block it with a polite laugh and denial. Try experimenting with letting the praise sink in and acknowledge to yourself that you have strengths that other people notice and like.

Activity 22: Ideas board

Start a bulletin board in the staffroom listing all the bright ideas everyone is putting into practice. Sharing talents, ideas and thoughts can help a busy teacher in many ways. Having a board that tells everyone about a new project or good websites for downloadable material, and so on, makes a valuable resource for the moments when you are looking for new ideas.

Activity 23: You make a difference

Know that you *can* and *do* make a difference. Some of the most rewarding moments in our lives as trainers and psychologists have been the times when adults have told us about the people who have 'made a difference' in their lives. So many times the people have been teachers they had at some point in their schooling – a person who believed in them, who encouraged them, who inspired them with passion for a subject, who was quietly supportive through difficult times. Those teachers remain in a person's memory long after the teacher has forgotten about the incidents that led to the fond memory being forged.

Activity 24: Make time for you

Do something at least once every week that you love doing. In an ideal world you would do something both in the classroom/workplace and in your personal time. In fact the more you do that you love, the more satisfied and stress-tolerant you will be. If you have been feeling jaded and burnt-out lately, you probably aren't having enough fun and fulfilment through doing enjoyable things. Think carefully about what you do love to do, what leaves you feeling exhilarated or replenished. Make sure these things are given priority in your diary. Perhaps start up a new hobby this term or rekindle old skills so that you spend time doing something you really enjoy.

Activity 25: The work–life balancing act

Make sure you have a well-balanced lifestyle. This links in with Activity 24. It is too easy to keep on trudging through each day exactly like the one before and ending up feeling depleted and de-energised. Check out your lifestyle. Have you got a work–life balance that is right for you? If not, take time during a weekend or when you are next on holiday to re-think your weeks and months, your priorities and activities.

Activity 26: Get to know people

Make sure all the staff in the school know your name and that you know theirs. In a large school it can be a bit daunting to try to get to know everyone, but it is worth the effort. A friendlier atmosphere will grow as people acknowledge one another. Your colleagues are your biggest source of support and you are theirs, so you need to develop those relationships as much as possible.

Activity 27: Check-up

Stop once an hour and let yourself look around, quieten your breathing. In a busy day, with a lot to get through, assessments to be completed and projects to get going, it is easy to forget to check whether you feel comfortable, tense, thirsty or hungry. It's worth checking these things regularly to make sure that your stress level stays as low as possible.

Activity 28: Give feedback

Let other teachers know the good things you have heard about their work. Colleagues are there at the coalface with you and deserve a helping hand from time to time. It can be a real uplift to have a piece of feedback from colleagues about some work that you have done and how they have seen it make a difference. Think how they would like to hear the same thing and start the ball rolling in the staffroom.

Activity 29: Don't be superman

Ask a colleague to give you a hand with a task. The culture in some schools is to pretend that you are superman/woman and can do everything easily and quickly without feeling any strain. This is unrealistic to say the least! Schools with a climate of mutual support work much better and tend to have less staff absenteeism through stress-related illnesses. What's the culture in your workplace? Do you want to change it?

Activity 30: Think positive

Develop a positive 'can do' attitude yourself. Teaching professionals who believe in themselves and show that they can tackle tasks and find solutions are good role models. More importantly they feel better about, and more satisfied with, their lives than people who avoid taking risks with new tasks.

DEVELOPING A SENSE OF SELF

This section provides an example of a programme to develop a sense of self.

Knowing what you want and getting what you want – the art of goal-setting

Introduction

In this programme the lesson plans all follow the same format and create a step-by-step development sequence, taking the users through a complete programme. In each lesson plan the lesson format is as follows (timings are approximate only and depend on the needs of the group):

- preview of session focus *(5 minutes)*
- review of last session *(10 minutes)*
- main activity *(15 minutes)*
- group discussion *(10 minutes)*
- personal reflection *(5 minutes)*.

The group discussions can include the following themes:

- What did you think?
- What did you feel?
- What can you use outside the group?

Session 1: Getting to know each other

Photocopy sufficient copies of Worksheet ☑, the 'learning log', so that each student has about 10 logs.

Aims

- To help participants get to know one another.
- To create a good emotional climate.
- To introduce the 'learning log' as a self-managed learning tool.

Task 1: Introductions

❖ Introduce the programme and the facilitator. Explain that the focus for these sessions is goal-setting and that this simple act can make a big difference to what people achieve. Give the students an example of a person like Oprah Winfrey whose motto is 'aim for the stars and hit the moon' and whose life story and ability to set goals and achieve them is obvious. Ensure that this example is relevant to the group.

❖ State that the participants must first get to know one another a bit better and that this will be achieved by playing a warm-up game.

Task 2: Playing detective

❖ Ask the students to form into pairs, choosing people they do not know well. They are not to speak to one another. Each person then draws four things that they have used over the last three months. Each item should be chosen so that it will help the pair to discover something about each other's interests. For example, someone who enjoys music might draw a CD. Remember it must be something *used*, not a picture of the interest itself. The drawings don't have to be great; in fact drawings that aren't very exact are funnier and good to share because the 'detective' has to be very intuitive and imaginative. Each person has a turn being the detective, while the person whose drawings they are looking at and talking about stays silent. After this, they can have a short chat with one another and also correct any misconceptions that may have arisen from the drawings!

❖ The whole group then comes together and each person introduces their partner by saying what they managed to discover about them. They can show the person's drawings to the group as they talk. Give 'permission' for everyone to take part in this and remind the students that they will all be feeling similar kinds of things. If the facilitator has a colleague present, they can introduce one another first to set the tone.

❖ Encourage general discussion while you ask everyone how they felt doing the exercise, what they thought about it and what they have learnt about themselves and each other through doing it.

Task 3: Ground rules

❖ This exercise works best after an initial warm-up activity, once the individuals have broken the ice with one another and are starting to gel as a group. It can be done through discussion and enquiry, inviting the group to form their own rules, or the rules can be suggested by the facilitator and the participants can agree or disagree in the discussion. The box below illustrates some typical ground rules agreed by such groups.

Typical ground rules

✔ Personal responsibility for what they discuss and what they do
✔ Respect for others' ideas
✔ No interrupting
✔ Anyone who is puzzled can talk to the facilitator after the group
✔ Confidentiality, if this is important and relevant

Task 4: Reflection

❖ Introduce the learning logs on Worksheet ☑2 and explain their purpose and use. They are a self-managed learning tool where the students take responsibility to reflect on what they have just experienced and make notes on the main learning points and possible future action as a result. Give each student a number of photocopies of Worksheet ☑2.

❖ Allow a few minutes for everyone to write down points in each section. Students can use a fresh copy of the learning log for each session and may photocopy as many as they need.

Session 2: What has been good in your life?

Aims

- To begin to learn what feels good and what feels unsatisfying.

Task 1: Preview and review

- ❖ Preview this session by telling the participants that today they will be looking at their life so far to find out what they feel good about.

- ❖ Next review the last session by doing a name reminder and asking the students in turn to tell the group which was their favourite interest out of the four they drew.

Task 2: My life

- ❖ Ask each individual to draw a pathway of his or her life so far, based on the following graph-style illustration which you could draw on a flipchart or board.

Happy/satisfied

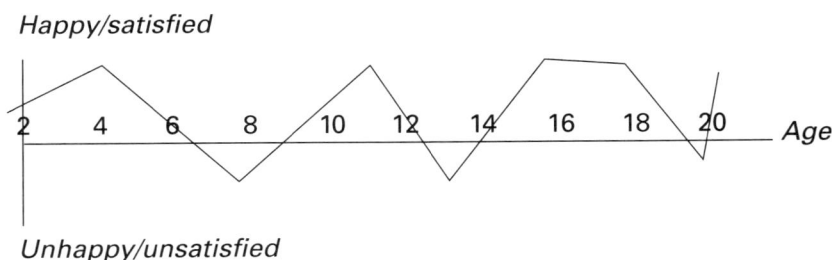

Unhappy/unsatisfied

- ❖ Ask the group to form into pairs or trios and to explain their drawing to each other as far as they want to. They can talk to one another about:
  - the things that they found satisfying in each time period;
  - what needs they had then that were being met;
  - what needs were not being met during times that were less happy and the drawing dipped below the line.

Task 3: Discussion

- ❖ Back in the large group again, discuss what they found. What were the kinds of things that made them feel happy and what made them feel unhappy? What needs did they have at different parts of their lives? Who or what helped them? What things would they like to achieve in the next period of their lives?

Task 4: Reflection

- ❖ Give everyone the opportunity to fill in their learning logs.

Session 3: What goals do you want to achieve?

Aims

- To free up the participants' thinking and widen their choices.

Task 1: Preview and review

❖ Preview this session by telling the students that today they will be starting to set goals – but they might be ones they have thought of before.

❖ Review the previous session by asking participants if they have had any thoughts about the exercise they did last time and remind them of how useful it is to know the things you enjoyed in the past when it comes to planning the future.

Task 2: In that case I would ...

❖ Ask the group to do the following exercise, writing down their responses. Read out each of the statements in the box below, and ask the participants to write down their responses to each, working individually at this point.

---

1. If the world were to end in the next 12 months, which three places would you visit before it ended?
2. Somebody has found the secret formula for a magic cocktail that, if you drink it, means that you cannot fail at anything you do. What three things will you do now you know that you will certainly succeed?
3. What job would you try out if you could choose *any* one in National Work Experience Week?

❖ Ask the group to form into pairs and discuss the ideas they had, asking one another questions such as:

- Do you know anyone who has done that?
- How did that person manage?
- What gave you that idea?

Remind them that each individual's ideas and dreams are special and deserve to be respected.

Task 3: Discussion

❖ Bring the students back into the large group and ask them to talk about the things they wrote and discussed with their partners. You can use the following questions as prompts if required:

- Are there several people with similar goals in the group?
- Do anyone else's goals inspire new thoughts in you?
- Do you think that you can achieve these things?
- How have the people who have achieved these goals done it?

Task 4: Reflection

❖ Give everyone the opportunity to fill in their learning logs.

Session 4: SWOT analysis of your goals

Aims

- To learn about a SWOT (**S**trengths, **W**eaknesses, **O**pportunities and **T**hreats) analysis.
- To start the planning process.
- To raise conscious awareness of strengths and hindrances.

Task 1: Preview and review

❖ Preview the session today by explaining that they will learn how to be a SWOT!

❖ Review the last session by asking them to talk about any thoughts or feelings they had after doing the exercise.

Task 2: SWOTS

❖ Ask the participants to choose the most important goal they identified in the exercise entitled 'In that case I would ...' (or to choose another big goal), and then find a partner. Together they will go through their goals, taking turns and helping one another to work out a SWOT analysis of the goal. Explain what 'SWOT' means (**S**trengths, **W**eaknesses, **O**pportunities and **T**hreats).

❖ Give out Worksheet 3 which contains the illustration below of such an analysis plus a blank template in which to analyse their own chosen goal. For this exercise the facilitator may have to go round the pairs to help them think of the different aspects of SWOT.

My goal: *To visit Prague and meet Codruta again.*	
Strengths I bring	• *Determination* • *£50* • *Knowledge of Geography* • *Memory of a visit in the past*
Weaknesses I have to think about	• *Often think of things but end up not doing them* • *Not good at saving*
Opportunities I might have to do all or some of my goal	• *My parents might go there again* • *Could find out about voluntary work there*
Threats or things that might get in the way of achieving my goal	• *Lose motivation* • *Spend all my money*

Task 3: Discussion

❖ Ask the group to come back from their pairs work and discuss the things they discovered about making their goal happen. Ask each person to tell the group what strengths they thought that they could bring to achieving their goal. Highlight the fact that some are personal qualities and some are tangible assets. Ask participants to help and encourage each other. If they have noticed a quality about another person that could contribute to their goal, encourage them to say what they think. Set the tone by giving some examples yourself from what you have learnt about each individual.

❖ Ask the students what they will do to help them make their goal happen now they have this extra layer of knowledge. Tell them that, in the next session, they will be learning about how they can help themselves even more.

Task 4: Reflection

❖ Give everyone the opportunity to fill in their learning logs.

Session 5: Thinking positively

Aims

- To help participants learn about the labels they give themselves.
- To help participants learn how to use positive labelling.

Task 1: Preview and review

❖ Start with a preview of the session and tell the participants that they will be learning how to re-program their brains! They might have noticed in the last session that one of their threats was their own personal lack of self-belief or negative thinking – this is why they will be 're-programming' themselves today.

❖ Review the last session by asking them to talk about any thoughts or ideas they have had about their SWOTs since they met.

Task 2: Helping myself

❖ Explain that sometimes somebody makes a comment about us when we are young and we believe it. We often then go through life believing that thing about ourselves. If that **label** were positive, it can help us a lot and become one of our strengths. But if it were negative, it can become one of those threats or weaknesses in our SWOT analysis. Give an example of your own here.

❖ Ask the group to work out the 'labels' that they have been given over the years – and may now attribute to themselves. A good way to find out what positive and negative labels we carry around is to answer the following statements:

Things I like about myself:
I am …
I am …
I am …

Things I don't like about myself:
I am …
I am …
I am …

A list of possible labels is provided in the box below to help with the exercise if needed.

Examples of labels
I am ... considerate, beautiful, attractive, kind, vibrant, funny, willing, persistent, trustworthy, cuddly, honest, cautious, clever, good with people, serious, positive, ambitious
I am ... lazy, careless, rough, unkind, silly, stupid, fat, ugly, sulky, negative, a moaner, gossipy, a big mouth, rude, untidy, a scrounger, bossy, reckless

Task 3: Discussion

❖ In pairs or small groups talk together about:
  • Any labels you share?
  • When do you think you were first labelled this way?
  • What labels would you like to change?
  • What labels would you like instead?

❖ Ask the students to reconvene in the large group to discuss the following questions:
  • What could I do to change the labels I don't like (and thus re-program my brain)?
  • How can I use the positive labels even more?

Task 4: Reflection

❖ Give everyone the opportunity to fill in their learning logs.

Session 6: How to get still further

Have some spare paper, sellotape and paper clips available for making paper planes during the exercise.

Aims

- To experience setting a target and making it specific and public.
- To learn to make SMART goals – ones that are **S**pecific, **M**easurable, **A**chievable, **R**ealistic and **T**ime-based.

Task 1: Preview and review

❖ Start with a preview by telling the group that they will be learning to fly today!

❖ Recap the last session by asking the participants to talk about any thoughts and ideas they have had since the last time. Remind them that they can make their own labels up and thus re-program themselves by telling themselves what they need to hear.

Task 2: 'SMART' moves

❖ Ask everyone to make a paper plane by folding up a sheet of paper. Test that these planes can fly! Next ask the students to fly the planes and record how far their own flew on its longest flight. They can work this out by paces or points in the room (for instance, as far as the leg of the table).

❖ Next the participants must estimate how much further they could make the plane go if they improve it using sellotape, paper clips, etc. They must write this down publicly on the board. This is their goal.

❖ Working singly or in pairs, they can work on the planes, improving them until they get close to their personally chosen target.

❖ Set up a final flight for all the planes and record the distances for each on the board next to the written aims.

Task 3: Discussion

* Use the following questions to prompt the discussion:
  * What did you feel when you set a new target?
  * Did stating it publicly make a difference?
  * What about those of you who had a partner? Did that make a difference? What was it?
  * Do you think your goal was realistic?
  * Are you satisfied with the flight of the modified plane?

* Draw out of the group that it makes a difference if they make SMART goals – ones that are **S**pecific, **M**easurable, **A**chievable, **R**ealistic and **T**ime-based. Write this up on the board.

Task 4: Reflection

* Give everyone the opportunity to fill in their learning logs.

Session 7: Achieving your goals in the future

Aims

- To finish the programme positively.
- To plan some actions for after the group has ended.

Task 1: Preview and review

❖ Preview this coming session by reminding the group that this is the last meeting and that they will be looking back over their achievements and saying goodbye to one another.

❖ Review the last session by asking them to talk about any thoughts or ideas they have had since they learnt how to 'get SMART'.

Task 2: I achieved ...

❖ Ask the group to divide into pairs or threes and take turns discussing the following points with one another. Remind the students to listen carefully to one another and encourage each other by suggesting things they think that person may have achieved that they may not have thought of themselves.
  - What did I hope to achieve by doing this programme on goal setting?
  - What have I achieved by doing it?
  - What am I doing differently as a result of what I have learnt?
  - What will I do differently in the future?

Task 3: Discussion

❖ Ask the group to reconvene as a large group again to discuss together what they have achieved. During the course of this discussion encourage positive and appreciative comments between the group members by asking them to think of who helped them most on this programme, who made them laugh most, and who they would like to help them achieve their next goals.

Task 4: Final reflection

❖ Give everyone the opportunity to fill in their learning logs.

DEVELOPING A SENSE OF BELONGING

This section provides an example of a programme to develop a sense of belonging.

Making friends – skills for getting on in life

Introduction

In this programme the lesson plans all follow the same format and create a step-by-step development sequence, taking the users through a complete programme. In each lesson plan the lesson format is as follows (timings are approximate only and depend on the needs of the group):

- preview of session focus *(5 minutes)*
- review of last session *(10 minutes)*
- main activity *(15 minutes)*
- group discussion *(10 minutes)*
- personal reflection *(5 minutes)*.

The group discussions can include the following themes:

- What did you think?
- What did you feel?
- What can you use outside the group?

Session 1: Getting to know each other

Photocopy sufficient copies of Worksheet [2] , the 'learning log', so that each student has about 10 copies.

Aims

- To get to know one another.
- To establish the ground rules.
- To introduce the 'learning log' as a self-managed learning tool.

Task 1: Introductions

❖ Ask the group to form a circle or sit so that they can all see each other. Explain that you are going to ask them to do a mime and to remember what each person's mime is.

❖ Ask each person to think of an interest they have that they can mime – it can be football, clubbing, reading, computer games or anything else that they enjoy. For example, if it is football, the mime might be showing everyone a ball and then miming a kick.

❖ The group is asked to remain quiet during each other's turns. Starting with either the facilitator or a nominated group member, each person mimes their own interest and everyone else tries to remember it.

❖ During the next stage of the game, the participants have to follow the sequence below:

Clap hands → mime own mime → clap hands → point to someone else → mime that person's mime.

The person who is starting first claps their hands and then mimes their own interest so that everyone can see it. They then point to someone else and, from memory, immediately do that person's mime. That person in turn mimes their own interest, points to a third person, mimes that person's interest, and so on. Give participants a chance to practise before going round the whole group.

❖ In the next round, people who hesitate or do the wrong mime are eliminated.

❖ At this point have a whole group discussion where participants have a chance to say how they felt about doing the activity and to talk about their interest. If people do not know one another this is a chance for them to introduce themselves by name.

Task 2: Ground rules

❖ This exercise works best after an initial warm-up activity, once the individuals have broken the ice with one another and are starting to gel as a group. It can be done through discussion and enquiry, inviting the group to form their own rules, or the rules can be suggested by you and the participants can agree or disagree in the discussion. The box below illustrates some typical ground rules agreed by such groups.

Typical ground rules

✔ Personal responsibility for what they discuss and what they do
✔ Respect for others' ideas
✔ No interrupting
✔ Anyone who is puzzled can talk to the facilitator after the group
✔ Confidentiality, if this is important and relevant

Task 3: Reflection

❖ Finish by introducing the learning logs, explaining their purpose and use. They are a self-managed learning tool where the students take responsibility to reflect on what they have just experienced and make notes on the main learning points and possible future action as a result. Give each student a number of photocopies of Worksheet ②.

❖ Allow a few minutes for everyone to write down points in each section. Students can use a fresh copy of the learning log for each session and may photocopy as many as they need.

Session 2: Speaking and listening skills

For this session you will need an object to represent the mace used in the House of Commons.

Aims

- To help the group get to know each other better.
- To build up confidence about speaking in the group.
- To start acquiring listening skills.

Task 1: Preview and review

❖ Start with a preview of this session by telling the students that today they will be talking and listening – these are the building blocks of good communication.

❖ Next, briefly review the last session by doing a name reminder and asking each person to remind the others what interest their mime was about.

Task 2: The mace

❖ Use any object such as a book, a pencil or a ball that can be passed around the group to represent the mace used in the House of Commons. Explain the rule for this exercise – anyone holding the 'mace' has the floor and can speak without interruption from the others. Everyone who wants a turn to speak can have one.

❖ Suggest the topic of friendship for discussion and remind everyone that the speaker is the one with the mace. You will be keeping a note of who has the mace and how often. Start the discussion off and keep a record as they talk. If necessary, remind the group about the 'no interruption' rule and help to keep the flow of debate going by asking questions such as:
- What do you think a good friend does?
- What are the qualities of a friend?
- Why are some people more friendly than others?
- What does an enemy do?

❖ After a while, stop the discussion and show the students your record.

Task 3: Discussion

❖ Ask the students the following questions to encourage a further discussion (without the mace). If you feel it is appropriate, you could address the questions below to the participants who were quiet during the friendship discussion in order to draw them in. Emphasise the importance of their contribution because they were able to listen and observe most.

- What does this tell you about the group?
- What does this tell you about different people?
- What does this tell you about yourself?
- Is this typical of how you often interact in a group?
- Do you want to change this?

❖ Point out that there were two types of contributions and identify these as the roles of speaking and listening. Emphasise that many people worry about speaking in groups or to other people, thinking that they won't be thought interesting, but that really the secret of good conversations, and therefore of making friends, is in listening.

Task 4: Reflection

❖ Give everyone the opportunity to fill in their learning logs.

Session 3: How well do you listen?

Photocopy sufficient copies of Worksheet 4 . (Alternatively, make sufficient copies of a passage of your choice, one that you think will interest the students.)

Aims

- To sharpen the participants' ability to listen.
- To create a shared experience to form the individuals into a group.

Task 1: Preview and review

❖ Start with a preview of this session by telling the group that today they will be listening and finding out how good they are at doing this. Ask the students how many of them think that they can listen well?

❖ Next give a brief review of the last session by asking them to contribute any thoughts or ideas they have had about having conversations with other people and building friendships since the last time they met.

Task 2: Chinese whispers

❖ Remind participants of the exercise in the last session where you highlighted the importance of both listening and speaking when they were with other people. Tell them that they will be doing another exercise today that will focus on listening. Ask them all, except one person, to move to the back of the room. (If the group has more than ten people in it, create two smaller groups.)

❖ Read the short passage from Worksheet 4 (or the passage of your choice) to the one remaining person. That person repeats what he or she has been told to the next person, and so on. After each person has their turn, give them the photocopied passage so that they can each note what had been added, missed out or changed by that point.

Task 3: Discussion

❖ After the game, discuss what had been left out and what had been changed in the passage.

❖ Draw out how often unfamiliar things, names, numbers and places are left out most quickly. If a word is misheard, the rest of the passage is often changed to make more sense. Some parallels with gossip could usefully be made and the impact that that can have on friendships!

Task 4: Reflection

❖ Give everyone the opportunity to fill in their learning logs.

Session 4: Body language

Aims

• To make participants aware of the power of body language.

Task 1: Preview and review

❖ Start with a preview of this session by telling the group that today they will be finding out what their unconscious body language conveys. Ask them why they think this might have an effect on friendships.

❖ Next give a brief review of the last session by asking what they thought about the last session and about listening since that session.

Task 2: Paying attention

❖ Ask the group to form into threes and to decide who is to be A, B and C. A is to talk to B about A's last holiday for 4 minutes. Take the people who are acting as B aside and tell them to look as bored as possible for the first 2 minutes, showing no interest in what A is saying. At the time signal, B is to change tactics and start showing interest and making comments. C is to observe what B does and what effect this has on A. What encourages A to talk more? What seems to stop A?

❖ Then ask the trios to discuss how it went together, using the following questions as prompts:
  • What was it like to be the talker?
  • What was it like to be the listener?
  • What worked?
  • What postures that B adopted made it easier for A?

Task 3: Discussion

❖ Ask the threes to form into the large group again to discuss this further. Ask the participants if they thought B acting as if he or she were depressed would have made a difference? Or acting happy? What does this tell you about the importance of listening and your body language?

Task 4: Reflection

❖ Give everyone the opportunity to fill in their learning logs.

Session 5: Negotiating

Aims

- To learn about negotiation.
- To practise listening as well as talking.

Task 1: Preview and review

❖ Start with a preview of this session by telling the group that today they will be going on an imaginary trip and learning about negotiating and co-operating.

❖ Next give a brief review of the last session by asking what they thought about the last session and about body language since that session.

Task 2: Dream holiday

❖ Tell the students that they are in luck! They have each won a dream holiday worth £500. Working individually, they are to write down where they would like to go, at what time of year and for how long, but should not let anyone else know what they have written at this point.

❖ Next ask them to write down six reasons why they want to go to that place at that time rather than anywhere else. Once they have listed six reasons, they must put them in order of priority by numbering them 1 to 6. They must still not let anyone else see.

❖ Now tell them that they have just run out of luck! They have no option about whom they go with and the competition organisers will allocate their travelling companion to them – and you are going to be the competition organiser. Allocate people to one another, choosing people whom you know have different interests and backgrounds.

❖ Tell them that they now have to negotiate a holiday for two that will cost no more than £500. They can talk about their own dream holiday at this point if they want to.

Task 3: Discussion

❖ In the large group after doing that exercise, go round the group asking the pairs the following questions:
- Where did you first want to go, and where did you end up?
- How much did the holiday you ended up with satisfy the six reasons you gave for wanting to do the original dream holiday?
- What was it like to negotiate with someone who had different ideas to you?
- How did you use your listening skills as well as your talking skills in this exercise?

Task 4: Moving human chain

❖ Ask all the participants to form into a line, all facing in one direction. Each person holds the waist of the person in front and then holds on tightly. The whole line has to lower itself to the ground without anyone letting go. They then have to move forward together by moving their feet forward in unison and then their shoulders. Finally, the group has to stand up together – all without anyone letting go.

Task 5: Reflection

❖ Give everyone the opportunity to fill in their learning logs.

Session 6: Compliments

Aims

- To help participants learn about giving and receiving compliments as part of their friendship skills.

Task 1: Preview and review

❖ Explain to the group that there is only this session and one more before the programme ends.

❖ Start with a preview of this session by telling the group that today they will be finding out about 'stroking' people – giving and receiving compliments! Ask them why they think this might have an effect on friendships.

❖ Next do a short review of the last session by asking what they thought about the last session and about listening, speaking, negotiating and doing things together since that session.

Task 2: Strokes for folks

❖ Explain that the group is going to learn about giving and receiving compliments – or giving and receiving 'strokes for folks'!

❖ Everyone sits in a circle. Explain how embarrassed people often are by saying something positive and complimentary to another person and that often it seems easier to criticise or say nothing, rather than to be positive. Psychologists think that receiving so many negative messages, or alternatively so few positive ones, can affect a person's self-image, so it is important to give your friends some compliments. Compliments are honest praise (also known as positive strokes). In this exercise each person is going to give a positive stroke to the person on their left. It must be something that they like about that person, it must be truthful and it must be about something that they do/have done, not about their looks or things that they can't control.

❖ The facilitator starts the process by saying to the person on his or her left: 'The thing I like most about ..... [name] is .... For example, 'The thing I like most about Emma is her gentleness with everyone she meets. She greeted everyone today with a smile and said something pleasant to them in a quiet voice.' (Don't talk in general terms; be sure to give a specific example. This will set the tone for the others and show them how to do this exercise well.) Go round the group, with each person complimenting the person on their left.

Task 3: Discussion

❖ Encourage general discussion and ask the participants how they felt at various points of the exercise. Embarrassment at both giving and receiving the compliments can be gently commented on as examples of how strange we find it in this culture – but that strangeness is not a good reason not to do it!

Task 4: Reflection

❖ Give everyone the opportunity to fill in their learning logs.

Session 7: Goodbye

Aims

- To finish the programme on a positive note.
- To have some plans for carrying on with the learning.

Task 1: Preview and review

❖ Start this last session with a preview by telling the group that today they will be saying goodbye to each other. Ask them why they think that saying goodbye pleasantly might have an effect on friendships.

❖ Next briefly review the last session by asking what they have thought about the strokes they received since that session.

Task 2: Reflecting on the programme

❖ This final session in the programme about friendship-making will be an opportunity to talk about the things that have made the greatest impression. Ask each person to give their contribution – either go round in order or let people talk as they feel ready. If people get stuck, the facilitator can use prompts such as:
  - the thing that was funniest;
  - the most interesting thing for me was;
  - what I would like to do more of;
  - the person who was kindest to me;
  - the thing I would most like to repeat;
  - the person who was a good friend to me during this time;
  - how I was a good friend during this time.

Let this discussion go on until everyone has said enough. People can talk more than once if someone else's comment strikes them as important.

❖ Ask the participants to talk more about what they will be doing differently now and to recall how they were when they started this programme.

Task 3: Reflection

❖ Give everyone the opportunity to fill in their learning logs.

Task 4: Group breathing

❖ Clear a space so that everyone can lie down in a circle with their heads pointing into the centre. They are to hold hands (preferably, and if they all feel comfortable with this) and shut their eyes.

❖ Ask them to concentrate as they try to breathe in and out at the same time as everyone else. After they have settled down, ask them to deepen their breathing as they start to relax but still to keep it in rhythm with the others.

❖ Say goodbye to one another.

DEVELOPING A SENSE OF PERSONAL POWER

This section provides an example of a programme to develop a sense of personal power.

Cool, calm and collected – how to choose the right response to people

Introduction

This programme is intended to help young people to develop and use different behavioural responses. Although it is specifically about developing an assertive response style, it also encourages them to work out what response style is best in any situation. In addition, this programme can help to improve the participants' levels of self-esteem.

For those who obtain vulnerable or low scores on the Self-Esteem Indicator, this programme offers a practical method to increase all three components of self-esteem, but especially the sense of personal power. Being able to choose an assertive behaviour option in many situations can be very helpful for many young people as it helps them to feel good about themselves and reduces stress. The teenage years are often plagued by a lack of self-esteem, so knowing about this option and using it fairly frequently can boost each component of their self-esteem. For example:

- Students' sense of self will be reinforced if they are able to act assertively in response to a request from a friend to do something they feel unhappy about. Those with a low sense of self will be helped by having time for self-reflection during the programme, and the use of a 'learning log' (see Worksheet 2 for an example template) will help participants make sense of what they are learning.

- Their sense of belonging will be increased as they will be better equipped to make and maintain friendships if they know how to be honest and straightforward in their dealings with other people. A low sense of belonging may also be increased through opportunities to work in pairs and small groups during the programme.

- If students are able to choose an appropriate behavioural response in a variety of situations and to communicate clearly, and thereby experience effective personal interactions, their sense of personal power will be enhanced.

However, a word of caution about assertive behaviour – sometimes speaking out honestly and firmly is not the best option – for example, there are times when criticising another person may cause unnecessary hurt. Making the decision about when to speak out is a judgement that each person needs to make individually. It depends on the time, the person, the situation and one's current priorities. In other words, acquiring these skills also involves learning to take the responsibility to think things through in each individual situation. For this reason, the programme emphasises opportunities to talk through the pros and cons of the different types of behaviour; it is also why each of the behaviours is called an 'option'.

Each of the nine sessions is based on a one-hour slot. However, all the activities may be shortened or extended as dictated by the time available, the students and the teacher. Approximate timings are given as a guide only and will vary according to the ages, skills, knowledge and particular needs of each group. Always allow an activity more time if it is going particularly well during the discussion time. Students often comment that they have too few opportunities to work and talk together like this.

Session 1: What's it all about?

Photocopy sufficient copies of Worksheets ②and⑤ . Each student will need about 10 copies of Worksheet ②, the 'learning log'.

Aims

- To introduce the topic of assertive behaviour.
- To introduce the main terms – passive, aggressive, assertive.
- To introduce the 'learning log' as a self-managed learning tool.

Task 1: What is assertiveness? *(10 minutes)*

❖ Introduce the group to the idea that you are all going to spend time learning about assertiveness over the next few weeks. Use the following information.

> Explain that being assertive is all about attitude, about having a win–win approach. To build and maintain win–win relationships, each person must accept responsibility for his or her own feelings, thoughts and behaviours. You cannot be responsible for the feelings of others, but you *are* responsible for what you say and do because your words and actions invite other people to feel certain emotions. Whether they experience those emotions or not is up to them.
>
> Assertiveness requires us to accept responsibility for our thoughts, feelings and behaviours *and* requires us to respect the thoughts, feelings and behaviours of others. When an individual accepts these responsibilities and stops blaming others for his or her feelings, a giant step has been taken toward a win–win philosophy.
>
> If you adopt an assertive response in some of the situations in which you find yourself, you will find that it is a way of behaving that allows people to deal with one another pleasantly but firmly. It can be used to show that you are not prepared to be unduly influenced by others and also that you don't want to lose friendships in aggressive arguments.
>
> It can be a very useful skill to learn if you find that you often get into arguments with other people or spend a lot of time avoiding unpleasant situations and feeling scared. However, like all other skills, it takes practice before you feel confident in using it.

❖ Encourage the students to suggest some examples from their own experience – either when they were assertive or when they feel they should have been.

Task 2: Situation A *(15 minutes)*

❖ Ask the students to get into pairs to discuss Situation A which is described overleaf and on Worksheet ⑤. *(5 minutes)*

> **Situation A**
>
> You have decided to confront your best friend whom you now know has been doing drugs recently. How are you going to tackle this?
>
> **Option 1:** You could get angry and have a go at your friend: 'You're stupid! Don't you try and involve me in this.'
>
> **Option 2:** You could find some time alone with your friend and say: 'I've heard you've been taking some pills. I feel worried that you are going to hurt yourself. What's going on with you? I feel like I've lost my best friend.'
>
> What is the difference between these two responses? Do you think one would be better than the other? Why? Why not?

❖ Bring the whole group back together to share their responses using the following prompts:
  • What is the difference between the two responses?
  • Would one response be better than the other?
  • Why? Why not? *(10 minutes)*

Task 3: Situation B *(30 minutes)*

❖ Ask pairs of students to read through and then to roleplay Situation B, which is described below and on Worksheet 5, enacting the three different responses. If this is the first time the group has done roleplay, you may find you have to give a lot of encouragement, especially to less confident students. After 5 minutes tell them to swap roles and try again. *(10 minutes)*

> **Situation B**
>
> Amy is walking down the hall at school. Her friend Vicki rushes up talking happily about a date with her new boyfriend. She asks Amy, 'Can I wear your new boots on Saturday? They'll look cool with my black skirt.' Amy doesn't want to lend out her new boots. What does she tell Vicki?
>
> **Option 1:** Stammering and blushing, Amy says, 'Oh sure, Vicki. You can borrow them.' Amy gets a stomach ache, goes home and feels sick all night.
>
> **Option 2:** Her face turns red and Amy says, 'I can't even believe you'd ask me that! You know they're my favourites and cost me a fortune. What makes you think I'd want to lend them to you?!'
>
> **Option 3:** 'Vicki, you're my best friend and I don't want to hurt your feelings, but those boots are special and I'm not going to lend them out. I hope you understand. You know, those new shoes and the red top you bought look great with that skirt and really suit you – you could wear them, couldn't you?'

❖ Bring the whole group back together to share their responses and discuss Situation B. They may also wish to share their feelings about doing a roleplay. *(10 minutes)*

❖ Now read out the descriptions of each type of behaviour in the box below, explain each and allow free discussion. *(10 minutes)*

> ***Option 1:*** When Amy reluctantly agrees to let Vicki borrow her boots, she's being **passive** – letting people walk all over her because she's afraid to speak up for what she wants.
>
> ***Option 2:*** Amy's angry reaction when her face gets red and she verbally 'hits' back at Vicki is **aggressive** – hurting people or putting them down because she doesn't know how (or is afraid) to honestly say what she wants.
>
> ***Option 3:*** The last response is **assertive** – Amy is straightforward and calm about telling Vicki how she feels and what she wants. She also adds a helpful suggestion as an alternative for Vicki that shows she is thinking about her needs.

Things to consider: Is dealing with people assertively usually your best choice? When might it not be?

Task 4: Reflection *(5 minutes)*

❖ Introduce the learning logs on Worksheet ② and explain their purpose and use. They are a self-managed learning tool where the students take responsibility to reflect on what they have just experienced and make notes on the main learning points and possible future action as a result. Give each student a number of photocopies of Worksheet ②.

❖ Allow a few minutes for everyone to write down points in each section. Students can use a fresh copy of the learning log for each session and may photocopy as many as they need.

❖ Encourage the students to manage their learning themselves by completing a learning log after each session.

❖ Finally, ask the students to be aware of their reactions to challenges during the next week, and let them know that you will be asking them about their experiences.

Session 2: How do you respond *now*?

Photocopy sufficient copies of Worksheets ⑥ and ⑦ .

Aims

- To describe where each participant is currently in relation to the different behavioural responses possible.
- To use this information to guide the amount of practice needed later in the programme.

Task 1: Recap of behavioural styles *(5 minutes)*

❖ Recap the previous session.

❖ Ask the group to tell you the differences between passive, aggressive and assertive responses.

Task 2: Behavioural responses quiz *(25 minutes)*

❖ Before learning how to develop their assertiveness, it is important for the students to take a few moments to get some idea of what they do now. Ask each participant to write 'Yes' or 'No' in the first column on Worksheet ⑥ (headed 'Yes/No'), depending on whether they honestly think that each statement is something they would be likely to say themselves. This will help them to gain insights about their own current preferred response styles. *(5 minutes)*

❖ Ask the whole group to discuss their general feelings about the questionnaire.

❖ Using the grid opposite to help you, work through the statements asking the participants to call out whether they think each statement is passive, aggressive or assertive. This may result in a brief debate for some statements while they work it out together. They then tick the correct answer in the columns on the right-hand side of their quiz paper. Then ask the students to compare their 'Yes/No' answers with the behavioural styles they have now filled in. From this they should be able to see if they use any styles in preference to others. *(15 minutes)*

Answers to the behavioural responses quiz		
Statement	***Style***	***Description***
1. Only an idiot would think of a solution like that! Don't you ever think before you talk?	Aggressive	Accusatory, exaggerated, blameful, invites defensiveness.
2. You know, maybe we might want to think about a different alternative. What do you think?	Passive	Hesitant, passive, apologetic, invites disregard.
3. Oh, I can't go – I have other plans.	Passive	Plans are only plans and can be changed. This is a subtle dishonesty and is one of the most common ways of avoiding having to say 'no'.
4. I'm not quite comfy with what you are suggesting. Let's try to come up with at least one more idea.	Assertive	Honest, respectful, invites co-operation.
5. No, thank you. I appreciate you asking, but I really don't enjoy that club.	Assertive	Honest, tactful, firm but appreciative (compare to statement 3).
6. Singing classes! You've got to be having me on!	Aggressive	Sarcastic, blameful, invites defensiveness.
7. This probably isn't what you wanted, but I guess I wasn't too sure about what you said. Anyway, I'm not very good at this kind of thing.	Passive	Self-deprecating, defensive, invites disrespect.
8. Well, OK, if that's what you want to do.	Passive	Hesitant, deferential, possibly dishonest about own wishes.
9. Great idea! Let's do it!	Assertive	Enthusiastic, genuine, co-operative.
10. Mum, please will you post that card I left on the table?	Assertive	Direct, respectful, invites co-operation.

❖ Finally, ask the group to think about times when each of the styles might be useful (that is, recognise that both passive and aggressive options have their place). *(5 minutes)*

Task 3: Assertiveness quiz *(30 minutes)*

❖ Hand out the assertiveness quiz on Worksheet ⑦ and ask the students to complete it. (Do not give them the results until they have answered the quiz.) Ask them to total up their scores and then to reconvene in the group once they have finished. *(10 minutes)*

❖ Now tell the students what the scores mean using the category descriptions below. As you read out what the different scores mean, ask them to put up their hand if they fall into that category. *(5 minutes)*

Scores for assertiveness quiz

If your total is **61 or higher**, you have a consistently assertive philosophy and probably handle many situations well. You may receive some ideas from this programme to further improve your skills and effectiveness.

If your total is **46 to 60**, you have a fairly assertive outlook. There are some situations in which you may be naturally assertive, but the programme will help you to increase your assertiveness through practice.

If your total is **31 to 45**, you seem to be assertive in some situations but your natural response is either non-assertive or aggressive. Using the suggestions in this programme to change some perceptions and practising new behaviours should allow you to handle things much more assertively in the future.

If your total is **15 to 30**, you have considerable difficulty being assertive. If you follow the suggestions outlined in this programme, practise and allow yourself time to grow and change, you can become much more comfortable in situations where asserting yourself is important.

❖ Talk through each of the statements on the quiz and ask:
  • Would that be easy or hard for you to say?
  • Who might you say that to?
  • What sort of response would they have?
  • How could you convey the same sort of message but say it in more 'everyday' language? *(15 minutes)*

Session 3: Programming yourself for success

Photocopy sufficient copies of Worksheets ⟨2⟩ and ⟨8⟩.

Aims

- To learn about the importance of self-talk.
- To learn how to change an internal belief pattern.

Task 1: Recap *(5 minutes)*

❖ Start with a brief recap of the previous session.

❖ Ask the students to tell you of situations and experiences they have had since you last met together. Who have they seen managing different situations well? What have they learnt from this?

Task 2: Positive mental imagery *(10 minutes)*

❖ Tell the group that today they will learn a useful technique to help them change their responses very effectively. Then describe **positive mental imagery** to the group in the following way. *(5 minutes)*

> Positive mental imagery is an exercise that requires you to concentrate. It is a way to influence your subconscious mind, which is a very powerful ally. Subconscious expectations and the words we use when we talk to ourselves are powerful influences on us. They influence how we see the world and how we feel from minute to minute. Much of what exists in our subconscious was 'recorded' in our early life and can be thought of as a 'psychological program', just like a computer program where the instructions are coded inside the software.

Explain that it is possible to change these programs using the techniques that will be learnt in this session. It will be fun because the students will learn how to design a 'psychological program' to help them every day.

❖ Discuss with the participants the ways in which they may be programming themselves to be passive, assertive or aggressive. Ask them to think about the things they say to themselves or other people. Do they tend to say 'I can't do that' when they are faced with something new? Do they tend to say 'He's stupid' if they don't get on with or agree with someone else? Do they tend to say 'What she wants is more important than what I want' or do they think to themselves 'I don't care about him, I'm the one that matters'? *(5 minutes)*

Task 3: How to re-program yourself *(30 minutes)*

❖ Use the information in the box below to explain that we can be 're-programmed' to some extent and how we can go about it. *(5 minutes)*

> Much of our original 'psychological programming' has been with us from childhood and it is this that makes us behave in our typical response style of passivity, assertiveness and/or aggression. We cannot remove the original programming, but we can insert some new programming to counteract it. So, unlike a computer, a person cannot be totally re-programmed. For example, with a computer, it is possible to create a new program and run it immediately. The computer does not have to 'unlearn' old habits. With people, new programming must be done gradually and the new 'program' must be 'run' numerous times before things become automatic. But, it *can* be done – so let's DO IT!
>
> To create a plan that will help you to re-program yourself, first write out new statements that will counteract old behaviours. These statements should be phrased in the following ways:
>
> - It's OK to ....
> - I can...
> - I will..
> - I am ....
>
> These statements must be written in a simple, active and positive form. If they are complex, passive or negative, you will not get good results (for example, you should write 'I am a positive person' rather than 'I will try to be less negative every time I speak').
>
> Start with only four or five re-programming statements. Write each statement on a small card so that you can easily carry them around with you. If possible, set them up on your computer as reminders so that they open each time you enter your email system.

❖ The students should work independently for this activity. Ask them choose up to five statements from Worksheet ⑧ that are most meaningful to them, or to make up their own statements. These should be written in their 'learning log', copied from Worksheet ②, ready to be used as homework after this session. *(20 minutes)*

❖ Ask the students to form into the group again. Discuss the statements they have chosen. Remind them that they could also make up their own if they thought of ones that suited them better. *(5 minutes)*

Task 4: Using the statements to get the best results *(5 minutes)*

❖ Explain how to use the statements to the best effect, using the information in the box below.

> To use the re-programming cards most effectively, you should be relaxed. To achieve deep relaxation you can enjoy a hot bath, listen to soothing music or rest after some hard exercise. Once relaxed, read each card aloud several times – hear the words, believe them, let them sink into your relaxed mind.
>
> Inserting ideas into your conscious, but highly relaxed mind will help you open your *subconscious* to receive the input. 'Programs' are stored in our subconscious mind and you must 're-program' your subconscious before it can support your new actions.
>
> Read your cards regularly for several weeks to condition your mind. You can read your cards at any time for additional reinforcement and, if you use the 're-programming' routine before you go to sleep, it is particularly powerful because your subconscious is active periodically during sleep (that's why we dream). Your subconscious will absorb what your conscious mind heard before you sleep if you use the routine regularly.

❖ Recap the simple steps to re-program yourself:
  1. Write down simple, active, positive statements (one per card).
  2. Achieve a state of deep relaxation.
  3. Read each statement aloud several times.
  4. Sleep and let your subconscious absorb the ideas.
  5. Do this daily for 3 weeks.

Task 5: When to re-program *(10 minutes)*

❖ Ask the students to form a pair with someone they have not yet worked with or don't know well. Ask them to discuss how they will use the cards and re-program themselves. Their task is to identify the best and most practical times at which they can do their re-programming. *(5 minutes)*

❖ For the rest of the session, discuss situations in which the students find it hard to come up with the best response. Note these on a flipchart, ready to use in the next session. *(5 minutes)*

Session 4: Recognising how you feel and talking honestly about it

Photocopy sufficient copies of Worksheet ⑨ .

Aims

- To learn about the importance of feelings in choosing a good behavioural response.
- To learn how to label feelings.

Task 1: Recap *(5 minutes)*

❖ Ask the participants to discuss how they have got on with their re-programming statements. Have they been using them? When? What has worked and what hasn't? Who needs help to find better statements or better times to do the re-programming?

Task 2: Why is it important to be honest about feelings? *(5 minutes)*

❖ Explain that, in this session, the group is going to learn about another key skill in being assertive – recognising what you feel and talking honestly about it. Ask the students why they think this might be important and encourage responses such as 'It helps us know what we like and what we don't like' and 'It helps people understand us better when we speak to them'.

Task 3: Talking about feelings *(20 minutes)*

❖ Describe how an important part of developing assertiveness is expressing your honest emotions appropriately. *(5 minutes)*

> Many people do not express their feelings honestly and appropriately. Even if you understand that being emotional is OK and part of being human, you may need to practise talking about your feelings. The assertive way to express feelings is to begin with 'I feel ...', 'I felt ...', 'I'm feeling ...', 'I am...', 'I was ...', 'I get ...'. What follows each phrase is a word describing a feeling.
>
> First you must know what you are feeling. To figure out which emotion you are experiencing, ask yourself, 'What am I feeling – mad, sad, glad or scared?'. These are the four basic human emotions and this question is a good one to help you get in touch with your feelings quickly and accurately. Some feelings are combinations of two or more of the four categories.

- Using the situations the group came up with at the end of Session 3, ask them to talk about what feelings they would be experiencing on each of those occasions. Remind them, if necessary, to discuss the times when they would have a mixture of feelings. Write the four basic feelings as column headings on the board (that is, mad, sad, glad, scared), and ask the group to tell you under which heading the words they are giving you should go. *(15 minutes)*

Task 4: What feelings do you have? *(30 minutes)*

- Hand out Worksheet ⑨ and ask the group to work in pairs to identify the feelings that they experience most frequently. Remind them to notice if the words/feelings fall under one or more headings. Invite them to add to the list if they come up with other words, and they can also add the words that came up during Task 3. *(10 minutes)*

- Now ask them to discuss their findings in the large group. *(5 minutes)*

- Looking at their lists, encourage the students to see if they have different sets of feelings in different settings – at home, at school, clubbing, in the playground, with adults in authority, with younger children. *(5 minutes)*

- Again ask them to discuss their observations in the big group. *(5 minutes)*

- Finally, ask the group which sets of feelings are associated with passive behaviour, assertive behaviour and aggressive behaviour. Mark these on the board using different colours. *(5 minutes)*

Session 5: Assertive talk

Photocopy sufficient copies of Worksheet ⑩ .

Aims

- To learn ways to phrase statements in order to make our communications more honest and more assertive.
- To identify situations during the next 24 hours in which participants could use the different responses they have learnt.

Task 1: Recap *(10 minutes)*

❖ Recap the previous session with the group. Ask if they have noticed themselves using feeling words more frequently since the last session. Also recap on the meanings of assertive, passive and aggressive behaviours and run through an example of each behaviour response with the group, asking for an example that somebody has seen or experienced during the last few days.

Task 2: Choosing assertive words *(30 minutes)*

❖ Explain that the group is ready to practise assertive responses now that everyone has a wider range of feeling words and a more positive program running internally. *(5 minutes)*

> There are ways to phrase the things you say that give a strong and firm, yet polite and respectful tone to your conversation. For example, you need to communicate thoughts, feelings and opinions assertively by choosing words that are direct, honest, appropriate and respectful. Some words simply do not fit these criteria and therefore cannot be delivered assertively. Words are only one aspect of being assertive, and we will shortly be looking at another very important part – body language – but words come first for now.

❖ Go through each example on Worksheet ⑩ , asking the participants to tell you into which category each statement falls (that is, assertive, passive or aggressive). Ask students what they think before telling them the answer given below. After the first two examples, the group can work in pairs to come up with a further example, showing a different type of response, which they then write on their worksheets. *(20 minutes)*

Guidelines for choosing assertive words: answers to Worksheet [10]

1. Use 'I' statements rather than 'you' statements.

Compare the following:

'You always interrupt my stories!' (Aggressive)

'I would like to tell my stories without interruption.' (Assertive)

Pairs to create a statement showing a passive response.

2. Use factual descriptions instead of judgements or exaggerations.

Compare the following:

'If you don't change your attitude, you're going to be in real trouble.' (Aggressive)

'If you continue to arrive after 9am, I will be required to give you a written warning.' (Assertive)

Pairs to create a statement showing a passive response.

3. Express thoughts, feelings and opinions reflecting ownership.

Compare the following:

'He makes me angry!' (Passive; denies ownership of feelings)

'I get angry when he breaks his promises!' (Assertive; owns feelings)

'The only sensible thing to do is go and sort them out, know what I mean!' (Aggressive; controlling, states opinion as fact)

'I believe that we need to go and talk to them about using our area for their football game.' (Assertive; owns opinion)

'Don't you think we should leave this for now?' (Passive; indirect, denies ownership)

Pairs to create another aggressive statement.

4. Use clear, direct requests when you ask others to do something rather than hinting, being indirect or presuming.

Compare the following:

'Would you mind taking this to Gita?' (Passive; indirect, only inquires about willingness)

'Will you please take this to John.' (Assertive request)

'Why don't you stop on the way home and pick up milk?' (Passive; indirect, asks the other to think about doing it or not doing it)

'Will you please pick up milk on your way home?' (Assertive request)

Pairs to create another aggressive statement.

❖ Explain that people avoid being direct and honest because they have previously learned to think it is impolite or 'pushy'. Unfortunately, while attempting to avoid being pushy we sometimes choose words that communicate a lack of respect. Sometimes we are so careful that we don't communicate the real message. You can give the following examples.

Examples

When we say, 'Don't you think …' instead of 'I think …', we are communicating indirectly and the words can sound condescending and a little manipulative. A more honest way to say it would be to take ownership of your own opinions about the subject and say, 'I think that buying her a bracelet is the best idea'.

When you ask, 'Why don't you …?' instead of 'Will you …?', you are actually asking a person to find a reason not to do something. So, if you say, 'Will you come with me to the cinema?' rather than 'Why don't you come with me to the cinema?', you will have talked in a direct, clear manner to the other person and he or she can give you a clear and direct answer in return.

If you say, 'I need …' or 'I want …', try adding a request as well so that you are clear about what you are communicating. 'I need to have that report in by Wednesday' would then become 'I need that report in by Wednesday. Will you give it to me on Wednesday morning?'.

These may seem like 'picky' details. You might think that most people know what is meant when you use those words – so what's the difference? The difference is that you may only be getting the results you hope for because people are able to figure out your unexpressed intentions. You may not be getting their respect. Continuing to use improper words will reinforce old habits and interfere with your relationships. It will be helpful if you practise using a range of options and notice what results you get. Notice particularly the responses you get when you use direct, honest, assertive words.

Invite discussion about this. *(5 minutes)*

Task 3: Identify situations *(15 minutes)*

❖ Use the rest of the time in the session to invite the participants to write down in their learning logs examples of situations that are likely to happen in the next 24 hours where they could use different responses. If time allows, they could roleplay the situation with a partner.

Session 6: Body language

Photocopy sufficient copies of Worksheet 11 .

Aims

- To learn about the body language behind each of the behavioural responses.
- To practise different ways of coming across to other people.

Task 1: Recap *(10 minutes)*

❖ Begin with a recap of the previous session. *(5 minutes)*

❖ Ask for examples of when the students used different responses and what results they got when they used them. Encourage them to discuss this in detail in the whole group. *(5 minutes)*

Task 2: What is body language? *(10 minutes)*

❖ Reinforce the message that people's choice of words is critically important, but perhaps how you say them is even more essential. A person's delivery of the message makes all the difference. Most people use the phrase 'body language' to refer to all the aspects of interpersonal communication beyond the choice of words. Everything becomes important when a message is being delivered.

❖ Ask the group what they think 'body language' is and encourage the following responses: tone of voice, volume, inflection, pace, eye contact or lack of it, facial expression, gestures, movements or lack of them, posture, muscle tension, changes in skin colouring, choice of clothing, hairstyle, glasses, etc.

❖ Explain the following.

> Staying aware of all aspects of body language continuously is not possible. Having some awareness is very important in your assertiveness training. Even though other people might not be able to list all of your body language signals during your interaction, they respond and interpret them unconsciously as part of receiving your message. This process is automatic, constant and complex.
>
> Don't be discouraged. You don't have to constantly monitor all aspects of body language in order to be assertive. You do, however, need to learn some body language signals to accompany your words that will help you to be perceived as an assertive person. You don't have to be 'perfect' at this to be successful!

Task 3: Body language signals *(15 minutes)*

❖ Give out Worksheet ⑪ . Explain that it describes some basic body language signals and categorises them according to how most people perceive them.

❖ Ask the students to go through the list first on their own. As they read the list, they may want to 'act out' each one to get a better sense of what the signal communicates. *(5 minutes)*

❖ Then ask the participants to form into threes to rehearse each of the signals. One person takes one minute to roleplay a passive person, including the posture, voice and gestures mentioned in the list while the other two people observe: one suggests ways to do it more convincingly and the other praises the things that the 'actor' has done particularly well. Then swap over to give the other people an opportunity to convey an assertive person and take a different observer role. Finally, roleplay the last response with everybody changing roles again. *(10 minutes)*

Task 4: Classifying body language *(10 minutes)*

❖ Ask the group to either form into pairs or stay in a large group as you read out or act out each of the descriptions below. 'Given the list of body language signals on Worksheet ⑪ , how would you classify the following – passive (non-assertive), aggressive or assertive?'

Description	Answer
1. Elbows out, fists on hips.	Aggressive. This posture makes a person look larger, much like birds fluffing out their feathers.
2. Touching someone's forearm as you speak with them.	Assertive. This may be a comforting gesture or a way to communicate emphasis.
3. While walking, putting an arm around someone's shoulders and firmly grasping their shoulder that is furthest away from you.	Aggressive. This entraps the other person and is a controlling manoeuvre rather than an affectionate or comforting one.
4. Shifting repeatedly from one foot to the other while standing.	Passive. The shifting movement communicates anxiety.
5. Constantly nodding head up and down.	Passive. Head-bobbing usually signals 'I want to please you'. Occasional nods may communicate attentiveness.
6. Leaning back, propping feet on desk, grasping hands behind head.	Aggressive. Most people perceive this as a power display.

7. Looking at toes while speaking.	Passive. Looking down frequently or steadily communicates anxiety.
8. Leaning forward with hands grasped, elbows on knees while seated facing someone.	Assertive. This probably will signal interest and attentiveness.
9. Rapidly tapping pencil (like a drumstick) while listening.	Aggressive. Tapping can communicate impatience or boredom, or it might come across as nervousness in a different context such as prior to an exam.
10. Sitting with elbows on table, hands together, chin on hands while listening.	Assertive. This looks relaxed and attentive.
11. Standing with arms folded while listening.	Aggressive. This is the most frequent interpretation. Others include 'closed mind', impatient, bored, uncaring and defensive.
12. Standing with arms folded, head tilted and legs crossed.	Passive or aggressive. This posture usually signals defiance and it is almost impossible to stay still. It could appear relaxed with a peer.
13. Looking over the tops of eyeglasses.	Aggressive. This signal usually looks disapproving or threatening.
14. Twirling a pencil with fingers at each end while talking.	Passive or aggressive. Twirling the pencil probably communicates anxiety. Doing it while listening to someone could signal impatience.
15. Elbows on table, hands together at fingertips forming a 'steeple'.	Aggressive. This is another subtle power display.

Task 5: Interpreting body language *(15 minutes)*

❖ Explain that it is important to understand that body language signals have many possible interpretations. A single body language cue is often not enough for an accurate 'reading' of the communication. Body language signals must be interpreted as a whole. Much like a detective, it is necessary to discover and interpret a number of clues to solve the 'body language mystery'.

Ask the group to brainstorm ways in which they could become better at reading body language. For example, one way to become more sensitive to body language is to become a 'people watcher with a purpose'. This can help you develop a better awareness of how body language communicates passive, assertive and aggressive behaviours. You will then start to notice that people not only use different words with each style, but also communicate these styles with different body language signals. Recognising passive and aggressive signals can help you learn to avoid using them when your goal is to be perceived as assertive. Another way is to find an assertive person and observe this person's behaviour, taking note of the words and body language used. Most of what we learned as children was through observation, and that system can still work. Following a good role model is an easy and fun way to learn how to become more assertive. *(5 minutes)*

❖ Think about people you all know and talk about the body language they display – use soap opera characters if you don't know many of the same people. Then think about each other – what is each person's most common body language? Does this fit with the earlier quiz on their habitual behavioural styles? *(10 minutes)*

Session 7: Practising assertive responses

Photocopy sufficient copies of Worksheets 12, 13 and 14.

Aims

- To start consolidating all the techniques learnt through practice.

Task 1: Dos and don'ts of phrasing *(15 minutes)*

❖ Give out Worksheet 12 and, as a group, consider the points highlighted under 'DO'. Then ask them to give you examples from their own experiences.

❖ For the 'DON'T' section, ask them to give you examples of different ways to convey the phrases.

Task 2: Time to practice *(30 minutes)*

❖ Tell the group to divide into threes, making sure that they are working with people they haven't worked with much so far. Ask them to select who will be Person A, B and C. Give them time to act out two roleplays chosen from the four situations described below and on Worksheet 13 . *(20 minutes)*

	Person A	**Person B**	**Person C**
First roleplay	Speaker who will act in an assertive manner.	Listener who will act in either a passive or aggressive manner (own choice).	Observer who will give feedback to the others about what he or she saw happening in the roleplay.
Second roleplay	Observer who will give feedback to the others about what he or she saw happening in the roleplay.	Speaker who will act in an assertive manner.	Listener who will act in either a passive or aggressive manner (own choice).

Situations

1. Someone is telling you what time the buses to the nearest town leave. You did not understand what they have just told you and you want them to restate the information.

2. You have a Saturday job and you believe you deserve a pay rise. You decide to ask your boss directly.

3. Your parents have invited you to come to a social event with them that does not interest you. Decline the invitation!

4. You are pleased about what someone has done for you. For example, your sister has cleared out a space in the garage for your bike. Tell her how you feel.

❖ After this exercise, come back into the group and discuss what that experience was like. Which role was easiest? What was difficult? How successful were they at finding assertive words and phrases? What did the observers notice about the assertive ones? Was it easier to be aggressive or passive as the listener? *(10 minutes)*

Task 3: 'Red lights and green lights' *(5 minutes)*

❖ Give out Worksheet 14 and go through the information about signals: 'Red lights and green lights'.

Task 4: Roleplay scenario using all the tips learnt *(10 minutes)*

❖ In pairs, invite the students to roleplay the scenario below using all the tips they have learnt so far.

> **Scenario**
> A teacher who is obviously in a bad mood tells you to do extra homework because you weren't able to answer the last question. You are the fourth person to be given extra work to do in that class. You think that the teacher is over-reacting and being unfair. What do you do and what do you say?

❖ Ask the group to come prepared to do more roleplaying and rehearsal in the next session.

Session 8: Advanced assertiveness techniques

Photocopy sufficient copies of Worksheet 15 .

Aims

* To learn advanced assertiveness techniques.

Task 1: Reviewing the group's behaviour *(15 minutes)*

❖ Ask the participants to discuss what they have noticed about their behavioural responses since the last session. Have they been using any of the options more or less? How have they found dropping words or sounds like 'y'know' from their sentences? Are there any situations in which they have found it easier to change their behaviour? Are the people they initially talked to about trying this different way of behaving still supporting them? Has anybody they have been talking to found their new responses difficult to deal with? Do some people seem to want them to go back to how they were?

Task 2: What to do when things go wrong *(30 minutes)*

❖ Teach the group the four steps to assertive communication – Steps 1 to 3 are covered in this session, while Step 4 is dealt with in Session 9. Introduce the four steps in the following way.

> We are going to look at things that can go wrong and what to do then. Even if you successfully choose effective words, correctly assess the other person and deliver your words with the appropriate body language, there is no guarantee that the other person will respond with the desired co-operative response! You never have more than 50 per cent of the control in any human interaction, and the other person may ignore all your skilful communication. Then what?
>
> This is when you need to be prepared to increase the power of your message. You should continue to be firm and polite, but become a little more insistent, a little more emotional or a little more commanding to be sure that you get what you want in the situation. Think of it as 'power steps' – you start at the bottom step, which is basic assertive behaviour and, if that does not work, you take one step up in power. If that does not work, you take another step and another, if needed. However this should not escalate all the way up to aggressive behaviour.
>
> So how do you do this? What is the next step up from a basic, polite response?

Now start to teach the first three steps to assertive communication.

Four steps to assertive communication

STEP 1: Repeat the question or statement

One way to add power to your assertiveness is to repeat your first communication. Some people have called this tactic 'broken record'. You ask the same question or make the same statement again. Make sure that you have good eye contact and that you speak with confident, firm voice tones. You may want to emphasise certain words the second time to increase the chances of getting your point across.

Assertive statement: 'Will you please tell me how to find Mr Green's class?' (No response from the other person)

Assertive statement: 'Will you **please** tell me how to find **Mr Green's** class?'

STEP 2: Command, don't ask

If the person continues to ignore you or refuses to co-operate, switch from asking to commanding. To most people a directive sounds more powerful than a request. If you make a request first, the average person will hear it as polite and appropriate – there is less risk of sounding pushy and it gives you the opportunity to change to a command if the request does not produce results.

Assertive statement: 'Please give me directions to Mr Green's class.'

❖ Before considering Step 3 and other ways to increase the power of people's assertiveness, use the situation below to allow the students to practise escalating their assertiveness just a little when their first effort is unsuccessful. Ask the group to form into pairs and try out the following exercise using what they have just learnt. *(5 minutes)*

> **Situation**
>
> You are participating in a school council meeting and want to ask a point about the topic being discussed. Choose a topic and write down your assertive statement. Alas, no one responds. Perhaps they have not heard you, or they may be choosing to ignore you. If you are going to repeat the original statement, write down which words you would emphasise to add a small amount of power. Still no one responds! Write down what you would say to be even more emphatic about your point without becoming aggressive.

❖ Come back into the group and each pair/several pairs talks through what they have written. *(5 minutes)*

STEP 3: Add emotion

If your efforts are still unsuccessful, expressing your emotions is another way to add power to your assertiveness. People are unaccustomed to others expressing emotion openly and honestly, and by doing so you add considerable power to your communication.

Assertive statement: 'Will you please tell me how to find Mr Green's class?' (No response from the other person)

Repeated assertive statement:	'Will you **please** tell me how to find **Mr Green's** class?' (Still no response)
Commanding assertive statement:	'Please give me directions to Mr Green's class.'
Assertive statement, expressing emotions:	'Now I'm getting cross! Please give me directions to Mr Green's class.'

❖ Discuss this with the group and reinforce the following points: *(10 minutes)*

- You will probably get some attention with the last statement!
- This level of assertiveness would be inappropriate earlier in the process but, after three attempts to be heard, it is quite appropriate.
- It may not only result in respectful attention, but may produce apologies from the others.
- You do not have to apologise for expressing your emotions and, in fact, it is recommended that you do not apologise.
- You are within your rights to respond emotionally if you do not receive respectful responses from others when you are making a serious effort to communicate with them.
- If you do receive the response you desired, try expressing appreciation.

❖ Tell the students that they will be covering the final Step 4 in the next session and that it concerns 'consequences'.

Task 3: Roleplay situations for trios *(15 minutes)*

❖ Ask the participants to form into threes to roleplay some of the following situations, which are also described on Worksheet ⟨15⟩ . Get them to swap around in the roles, with the third person as an observer each time to feedback comments.

> **Situation 1:** Your friend has taken your favourite pen to write some notes and has forgotten to give it back to you. You ask for it back and she doesn't respond.
>
> **Situation 2:** Your brother has told you he'll tell your mother that he has seen you smoking if you don't give him a fiver. You've asked him nicely not to do this and he isn't responding. What do you do next? What do you say next?
>
> **Situation 3:** Your tutor has asked you to bring in photographs to use in one of your projects and after a couple of requests to your mother she has still not looked some out for you. What will you do and say now?

Session 9: Practising assertive behaviour

Aims

- To learn the final step (Step 4) of assertive behaviour.
- To practise and consolidate the skills learnt.

Task 1: *(10 minutes)*

❖ Explain that, in this last session, the group will be learning the final stage (Step 4) of the advanced techniques for responding to others and will be talking over all the learning points. There will be time for more roleplaying and peer coaching if that is what the group wants.

❖ Ask whether they think they would answer the behavioural responses quiz in a different way now. Why? What has been the most helpful tip they have picked up? What do they now use regularly? What helped them change?

❖ Ask the participants to recall the first three steps to get the message across, that were covered in Session 8, as a lead-in to Step 4 – consequences.

Task 2: Assertive communication – the final step *(25 minutes)*

❖ Teach the group Step 4 of assertive communication.

STEP 4: Introduce consequences

A final way to add power to your assertiveness is to introduce consequences. Consequences are not threats, because they are not harmful or inappropriate. They are simply statements of what you intend to do if you do not get the co-operation or results you desire. Here are some criteria for giving successful consequences.

- Consequences need to be stated in advance. The other person deserves an opportunity to change his or her behaviour to avoid the consequence. Taking the action without prior notice could be interpreted as inappropriate and is likely to backfire on you when the other person becomes aggressive.
- Consequences need to be strong but believable. The action needs to be something that the other person does not want to experience, but if it is too extreme the other person will not believe that you will actually do it. Empty threats are likely to be ignored.
- You must be prepared to follow through and implement the consequence if necessary. If the other person decides to ignore your words and then you do not take the action you said you would, you will lose credibility and also the power to deal with this person in the future. He or she may also tell others, and you will lose credibility with them too.

- Talk through the following examples with the group and ask them to come up with some consequences that fit the criteria. Write the good ones up on the board. You can also tell the students the sample responses given below if needed. *(10 minutes)*

Examples

1. After several attempts to stop someone taking things from your desk without permission, what would you say?

   Sample response: 'If you take anything else from my desk without asking first, I will tell our tutor about this and show them the record I have kept of what you have taken.'

2. After you have asked your friend to drive within the speed limit in a built-up area where you know children play on their bikes, what would you say?

   Sample response: 'I really am uncomfortable with your driving so fast here. It's illegal and those kids are in danger. If you do this again I won't come out with you in the car again.'

Task 3: Practising introducing consequences *(15 minutes)*

❖ Ask the group to form into trios again to roleplay the situation below. Describe the situation to the students or write in on a flipchart. The observer will be looking to see which responses get the best reactions. *(10 minutes)*

Situation (in four parts)

1. Assume that you have purchased an expensive new suit for interviews. The purchase price included alterations. You were in a hurry and did not try on the suit when you picked it up after the alterations. The next day you discovered that the sleeves were still a little too long, there were a couple of wrinkles across the shoulders and the waist was a bit loose. You have decided to return the suit for additional alterations and expect this additional tailoring to be free. How will you word your first request?

   Sample answer: 'When I put on my new suit I discovered several things about the fit that are not quite satisfactory, so I brought it back for you to fix. Will you please take care of it for me?'

2. Next, you are told by the assistant that the additional alterations will cost another £35. What will you now say to get the assistant to provide the alterations at no charge?

   Sample answer: 'My understanding was that alterations were included in the price and that a good fit was guaranteed, so I would appreciate you making these few small adjustments without charge.'

---

3. Next, assume that this effort falls on deaf ears. The salesperson informs you that the store's policy requires payment for additional alterations after the customer has accepted the clothing, and he/she does not have the authority to break this rule. What will you say?

Sample answer: 'When I picked up the suit I explained that I did not have time to try it on, and I was informed that would be no problem. If I had tried it on then, I would not have accepted the suit as it is. If you cannot authorise additional alterations without charge, please fetch someone who can.'

4. Next, assume that this third attempt is also unsuccessful. What consequences will you now give the assistant?

Sample answer: 'If you will not get your supervisor to authorise this and if you insist on charging me for additional alteration, I will not shop here in future. However, I will inform your senior management about this incident, and I will also inform the editor of the Customer Hotline column in the local *Citizen* newspaper.

❖ Talk through this last scenario once the trios have roleplayed it. *(5 minutes)*

Task 4: Goodbye *(10 minutes)*

❖ Finish the programme by asking if there are any parts with which the participants would like extra help and ask if there is an occasion coming up where they think they will need to manage the other person carefully. Ask for suggestions for each situation and get the person with the situation to roleplay it with a friend in front of the group so that everyone can coach from the sidelines. *(5 minutes)*

❖ Tell the group that you will be following them all up in a few weeks to see how they are getting on and wish them well. Tell them what you have appreciated about their participation in the group – make sure your statement is clear, direct and uses 'I' language! *(5 minutes)*

DEVELOPING GENERAL SELF-ESTEEM

Example structure for a general self-esteem building programme

This section provides a description of the planning and design of a self-esteem building programme that incorporates the critical success factors outlined in Chapter 5, on page 31. The programme facilitator can extract the parts that are most helpful to the particular situation.

The initial preparatory stages are just as important as the later ones when delivering the programme. It is at this point that the thinking and planning are put in place to support the later work. The importance of having used the Self-Esteem Indicator prior to this stage can be seen. Most self-esteem building programmes omit to carry out any initial assessment in their eagerness to get on and do something concrete to help the students. This has the effect that meaningful evaluation cannot be made later because no baseline measures were taken. It also means that the essential focus is lost and the students receive generalised input rather than individualised material. Inevitably, a generalised approach will not be as effective as an individualised one.

Pre-programme checklist

Points 1 to 3 may be done in any order that seems appropriate to the specific circumstances.

1. Choose the individual or group.
2. Choose the facilitator.
3. Complete the Self-Esteem Indicator for each student.
4. Design the programme.
5. Prepare for implementation of the programme.

Content and processes of the programme

The programme design usually involves planning the content of the programme as well as thinking through the processes through which it will be delivered. The processes include the use of activities such as worksheets, pairs and trios exercises and large group discussions.

Processes also refers to the particular mixture of styles the facilitator will use during the programme. For example, a facilitator who spends a larger proportion of time teaching the skills and less time encouraging group discussion, who seldom offers the students choice, and who dictates the pace and content of each session, will have a different result to a facilitator who does the opposite.

The reason why self-esteem building programmes need to be facilitated rather than taught is because a focused, yet student-centred session allows the young people to experience more autonomy and space than normal. This opportunity allows them to draw learning from their experiences, rather than being told things. Since humans learn 87 per cent of what they know through experience as opposed to 13 per cent from what they hear, facilitation is a far better option for this type of learning (Mehrabian, 1976). Teaching professionals who are happier in the facilitator role will do well in these groups, while those who prefer to teach can be brought in to do some of the skills sections where their talents are particularly useful. It is important, however, to make it clear to these teachers that they may not inhibit the discussions that take place during the exercises and that these elements of the session will be the responsibility of the facilitator.

Delivering the programme

The delivery of the programme to a specified group typically follows the steps outlined below.

1. Introductions

Each person, including the facilitator, says hello and introduces themselves briefly. This starts to form a sense of belonging as everyone listens to one another and finds out areas where they have common experiences.

2. Defining self-esteem

- Introduce the concept of self-esteem, giving examples of behaviour, feelings and beliefs associated with high self-esteem and low self-esteem to make it personal and real for the participants.
- Feedback the results of the Self-Esteem Indicator (unless this has already been done in the pre-programme stage) to provide a focus for each individual.

3. Understanding self-esteem

- Outline what some researchers have said about self-esteem, emphasising that it is a feeling we have inside and it involves having a sense of self-worth.
- Define self-esteem in a way that is consistent with the theory you have espoused.
- Describe the three components of self-esteem in more detail to help the participants understand the meaning of their results on the Self-Esteem Indicator.

4. Increasing sense of self and/or belonging and/or personal power

This depends on the results of the Indicator. In this section participants need to be helped to make more connections with themselves and to get to know each other. Tackling activities that they are likely to find fun and easy will help them be less defensive, leading to successes that can be built on.

- Use self-awareness raising activities to develop a sense of self, such as Activity 16 'Let's have a debate' or a learning log (see Worksheet 2 for an example template).

- Share experiences and find commonalities to increase a sense of belonging through exercises such as Activity 18 to create a group 'Who's who' together.

- Draw out or roleplay some personal triumphs and talk about them to boost each person's sense of personal power. Use tasks such as Activity 12 'Guided visualisations' to open their 'inner' eyes to possibilities.

5. Increasing competences in sense of self and/or belonging and/or personal power

In this section of the programme more attention can be given to skill-building. The participants will have got to know one another better by this point and will be more willing to trust each other. Therefore, they should be more willing to take risks when they are practising new skills and more open to both positive and constructive negative feedback when they have completed a task. For example:

- Teach positive self-talk techniques or relaxation methods to help increase a sense of self.

- Teach active listening, empathy skills and social skills to develop a sense of belonging.

- Teach assertiveness skills and anger management, and practise problem-solving techniques to increase a sense of personal power.

6. Consolidating self-esteem

At this point the participants need to continue practising what they have learnt. They also need to keep having good experiences within the group to reinforce their learning. For the facilitator the focus moves from teaching new things to helping the participants reflect on their experiences and choose what they will do next. This means that the following issues will be dealt with in the sessions.

- Re-do the Self-Esteem Indicator.

- Review what was achieved during the programme by referring to the initial and current results on the Indicator.

- Each person develops their own action plan to continue to build the weaker self-esteem component or makes a decision to build on what is already relatively strong. It is best if the participants make this decision themselves since this will ensure that they have some commitment to continuing to develop themselves.

- Set up a peer-buddy system where each participant knows who their support buddy is with whom they can keep in touch and celebrate their changes.

- Teach the participants how to use the peer-buddy system effectively and set up a meetings schedule.

- Say goodbye to one another and the group to reinforce all three components of self-esteem.

Post-programme checklist

1. Evaluation of the programme content.
2. Evaluation of the programme process.
3. Re-assessment of the participants three to six months later using the Self-Esteem Indicator.

After the programme, the facilitator and the students need to implement their action plans. Facilitators can review what worked and what did not work so well, what they believe they did well and where they may want to gain more skills before making a second attempt. By using feedback from the students, and any colleagues who have been participating, facilitators can make a useful contribution to their continuing professional development. Ongoing, though reduced contact with the group is important. If some contact is not made the students will experience themselves as having been abandoned to their fate and may disengage from their new learning in defiance of the facilitator in whom they will have lost confidence.

For the students it is usually a time of challenge. They no longer have the security of their group, the supportive facilitator and the shared experience of being with others like themselves. They find themselves on their own, trying to keep up new habits and behaviours in the situations where they previously failed. This is a very tall order for them. It is very important that the facilitator has contact with the students once the programme has finished, and that they set up a peer-buddy system where each of the students has a friend to whom they can turn and get support. Regular checking in with their buddy, to update each other about their successes and difficulties, will help them keep on track and use what they have learnt. It takes more than 21 days' practice for a new behaviour to become a habit, so the first three weeks after a programme are critical ones for the participants if they are to be as effective as possible in their self-esteem development. It is helpful if a peer-buddy system with an agreement to support each other for at least 21 days after the programme is built into the post-programme planning.

WORKSHEETS

These worksheets are photocopiable. The worksheet required for a particular activity or task is specified in each activity or task's notes in the format 'Worksheet [1]'.

1 Who's who

1. My name is ....

2. I live in ....

3. I like to ....

4. My last holiday was ....

5. My favourite type of food is ....

6. My dream job would be ....

7. If I had one wish that would change the world for the better, I would wish for

....

....

This is a photograph of me:

2 Learning log

What happened?
What I learnt
What I'm going to do differently in future

3 SWOT

My goal: *To visit Prague and meet Codruta again.*	
Strengths I bring	• *Determination* • *£50* • *Knowledge of Geography* • *Memory of a visit in the past*
Weaknesses I have to think about	• *Often think of things but end up not doing them* • *Not good at saving*
Opportunities I might have to do all or some of my goal	• *My parents might go there again* • *Could find out about voluntary work there*
Threats or things that might get in the way of achieving my goal	• *Lose motivation* • *Spend all my money*

Your goal

My goal:	
Strengths I bring	
Weaknesses I have to think about	
Opportunities I might have to do all or some of my goal	
Threats or things that might get in the way of achieving my goal	

© Elizabeth Morris, 2002. All rights reserved. *Insight Secondary*, ISBN 0 7087 0356-9. Published by nferNelson. nferNelson is a division of Granada Learning, part of Granada plc.

Having got to bed at 4am after listening to bazooka music, Dimitri felt rough as he got up again at 7am. He had to go to Thessaloniki that day, leaving Volos at 8am and arriving for the meeting at 12.30. As he had a cup of strong Greek coffee and a plate of fried cheese for breakfast, he found the papers he would need for the meeting about the sale of his friend's, Mr Galanos, factory.

The bus was full and he saw that his old school friend, Phillipos Barouta, was also travelling to Thessaloniki that day. They sat together. 'Yasus' they said, and immediately started to talk about the times they went to Horefto to swim when they were boys. The bus used to take two hours they remembered. They would leave at 2.15pm and arrive at 4.15pm – as long as the road was clear of the big lorries taking apples to Athens. The time their bus had had to reverse down the corniche road to find a place where the two huge vehicles could pass was still in their minds, even 20 years later. 'We thought we were going to die – and so did that bus driver!' said Dimitri. Eventually they fell asleep after they had some ouzo and water at the rest stop halfway to the city.

Arriving on time, Dimitri went to the centre and had his meeting, talking and negotiating with the Demitriades brothers to make sure that his friend got the best price for his factory. The brothers wanted to expand their manufacturing facility and thought that Volos was a good place in which to start up. At 2pm they all went for lunch and drank retsina, ate dolmades and gigantes and finished off with a plate of fresh figs. There was no more talk of money then. They all knew that that would take more time and more talk. They would finish the business by winter. Dimitri thought that he had done a good day's work.

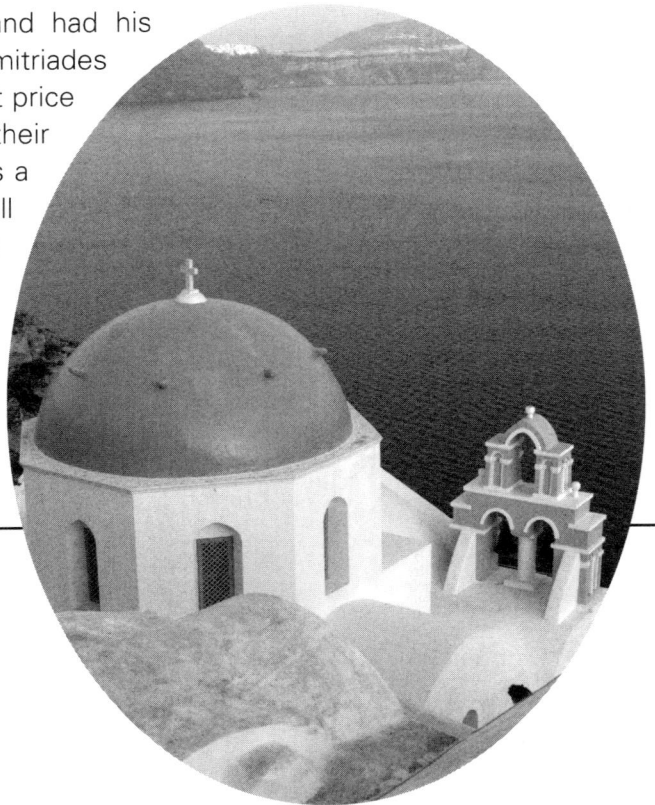

Situation A

You have decided to confront your best friend whom you now know has been doing drugs recently. How are you going to tackle this?

Option 1: You could get angry and have a go at your friend: 'You're stupid! Don't you try and involve me in this.'

Option 2: You could find some time alone with your friend and say: 'I've heard you've been taking some pills. I feel worried that you are going to hurt yourself. What's going on with you? I feel like I've lost my best friend.'

What is the difference between these two responses? Do you think one would be better than the other? Why? Why not?

Situation B

Amy is walking down the hall at school. Her friend Vicki rushes up talking happily about a date with her new boyfriend. She asks Amy, 'Can I wear your new boots on Saturday? They'll look cool with my black skirt.' Amy doesn't want to lend out her new boots. What does she tell Vicki?

Option 1: Stammering and blushing, Amy says, 'Oh sure, Vicki. You can borrow them.' Amy gets a stomach ache, goes home and feels sick all night.

Option 2: Her face turns red and Amy says, 'I can't even believe you'd ask me that! You know they're my favourites and cost me a fortune. What makes you think I'd want to lend them to you?!'

Option 3: 'Vicki, you're my best friend and I don't want to hurt your feelings, but those boots are special and I'm not going to lend them out. I hope you understand. You know, those new shoes and the red top you bought look great with that skirt and really suit you – you could wear them, couldn't you?'

6 Behavioural responses quiz

Read through the statements. Try to honestly say whether each is something you yourself would say. Write 'Yes' or 'No' in the column headed 'Yes/No'.

Ignore the other three columns for now – you will fill these in later as a group exercise to identify whether each spoken statement is passive, assertive or aggressive.

	Yes/No	Passive	Assertive	Aggressive
1. Only an idiot would think of a solution like that! Don't you ever think before you talk?				
2. You know, maybe we might want to think about a different alternative. What do you think?				
3. Oh, I can't go – I have other plans.				
4. I'm not quite comfy with what you are suggesting. Let's try to come up with at least one more idea.				
5. No, thank you. I appreciate you asking, but I really don't enjoy that club.				
6. Singing classes! You've got to be having me on!				
7. This probably isn't what you wanted, but I guess I wasn't too sure about what you said. Anyway, I'm not very good at this kind of thing.				
8. Well, OK, if that's what you want to do.				
9. Great idea! Let's do it!				
10. Mum, please will you post that card I left on the table?				

7 How assertive are you?

Assign a number to each item using this scale.

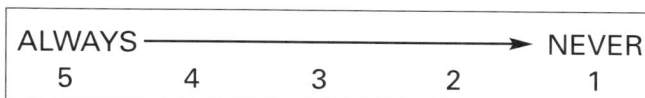

ALWAYS				NEVER
5	4	3	2	1

1. I ask others to do things without feeling guilty or anxious.	
2. If someone asks me to do something I don't want to do, I say 'no' without feeling guilty or anxious.	
3. I am comfortable when I meet new people.	
4. I confidently express my honest opinions to adults such as teachers, parents and my work placement boss.	
5. When I experience powerful feelings like anger, frustration, disappointment, etc., I can talk about them easily.	
6. When I express anger, I do so without blaming others for 'making me mad'.	
7. I am comfortable speaking up in a group situation (such as at a meeting).	
8. If I disagree with the majority opinion of my friends, I can 'stick to my guns' without feeling uncomfortable or being horrible to anyone.	
9. When I make a mistake, I own up.	
10. I tell others when their behaviour creates a problem for me.	
11. I feel comfortable when meeting new people in social situations.	
12. When I discuss the things I feel strongly about, I do so without labelling the opinions of others as 'crazy' or 'stupid'.	
13. I assume that most people are competent and trustworthy and I do not have difficulty asking different people to help me when I need it.	
14. When considering doing something I have never done before, I feel confident that I can learn to do it.	
15. I believe my needs are as important as those of others.	
Total score (add up the numbers you assigned to each item)	

The most important statements are those that will help you change old patterns of thinking and behaving. You are the person who is best equipped to identify what you want and need to change, and to create a new program to support this change.

Below are some examples of good positive re-programming statements. Begin with these. Once you have got these statements working for you, you may then want to use others that you make up yourself.

Choose four or five of the statements below – the ones that are the most meaningful to you – and focus on them.

- It's OK for my wants and needs to be as important as those of other people.
- I can get my needs met.
- I will ask for what I want.
- I will tell people what I don't want or like.
- I am someone who deserves to have my needs met.
- It's OK to feel what I feel and express this appropriately.
- I can express my feelings openly and honestly.
- I will tell others what I am feeling.
- I am an emotionally honest person.
- It's OK to make mistakes or to not know something.

- I can admit my mistakes or say 'I don't know'.
- I will admit my mistakes and say 'I don't know' when asked.
- I am honest and will learn from my mistakes.
- I can allow others to make mistakes.
- I will have reasonable expectations of others.
- I am realistic and understand that everyone makes mistakes.
- It's OK to experiment with trusting others.
- I am a trusting and sharing person.
- I am creative and can find good solutions to difficulties.
- I am a good communicator.

Now, if you wish, write some simple, positive statements for yourself. They can be in any of the forms shown, but the ones starting with 'I am …' are probably the most powerful.

Affirmation

I am ....

I am ....

Permission

It's OK to ....

It's OK to ....

I can ....

I can ....

Commitment

I will ....

I will ....

© Elizabeth Morris, 2002. All rights reserved. *Insight Secondary*, ISBN 0 7087 0356-9. Published by nferNelson. nferNelson is a division of Granada Learning, part of Granada plc.

9 Identifying your feelings

The following list may help you to find words to express your feelings in a direct, open and honest manner. You can add to the list if you come up with other words. Remember that each person experiences feelings in a different way, so you might put the word under a different heading to your partner. For example, some people use the word 'upset' to mean 'mad', while to others it means 'sad'.

Mad	Sad	Glad	Scared	Combinations
irritated	unhappy	pleased	anxious	guilty
annoyed	disappointed	happy	worried	jealous
angry	despondent	joyful	fearful	frustrated
ticked off	blue	delighted	concerned	embarrassed
furious	hurt	effervescent	afraid	uncomfortable
miffed	grief	comfortable	nervous	confused
upset	down	up	inhibited	perplexed
fuming	lonely	excited	uncertain	torn

1. Use 'I' statements rather than 'you' statements.

Compare the following statements and write down the type of response you think has been used in each.

'You always interrupt my stories!' ....

'I would like to tell my stories without interruption.' ....

Add another statement showing a passive response: ....

....

2. Use factual descriptions instead of judgements or exaggerations.

Compare the following statements and write down the type of response you think has been used in each.

'If you don't change your attitude, you're going to be in real trouble.' ....

'If you continue to arrive after 9am, I will be required to give you a written warning.' ....

....

Add another statement showing a passive response: ....

....

3. Express thoughts, feelings and opinions reflecting ownership.

Compare the following statements and write down the type of response you think has been used in each.

'He makes me angry!' ....

'I get angry when he breaks his promises!' ....

'The only sensible thing to do is go and sort them out, know what I mean!' ....

'I believe that we need to go and talk to them about using our area for their football game.' ....

....

'Don't you think we should leave this for now?' ....

Add another statement showing an aggressive response: ....

....

4. Use clear, direct requests when you ask others to do something rather than hinting, being indirect or presuming.

Compare the following statements and write down the type of response you think has been used in each.

'Would you mind taking this to Gita?' ....

'Will you please take this to John?' ....

'Why don't you stop on the way home and pick up milk?' ....

'Will you please pick up milk on your way home?' ....

Add another statement showing an aggressive response: ....

....

Non-assertive/passive body language

Posture
Slumped
Shoulders forward
Shifting often
Chin down
Sitting legs entwined

Gestures
Fluttering hands
Twisting motions
Shoulder shrugs
Frequent head-nodding

Facial expression
Lifted eyebrows, pleading look, wide eyes, rapid blinking
Nervous or guilty smile
Chewing lower lip
Shows anger with averted eyes, blushing, guilty look

Voice
Quiet, soft, higher pitch
Uhs, ahs, hesitations
Stopping in 'midstream'
Nervous laughter
Statements sound like questions, with voice tone rising at the end

Assertive body language

Posture
Erect but relaxed
Shoulders straight
Few shifts, comfortable
Head straight or at slight tilt
Sitting legs together or crossed

Gestures
Casual hand movements
Relaxed hands
Hands open, palms out
Occasional head-nodding

Facial expression
Relaxed, thoughtful, caring or concerned look, few blinks
Genuine smile
Relaxed mouth
Shows anger with flashing eyes, serious look, slight flush of colour

Voice
Resonant, firm, pleasant
Smooth, even-flowing
Comfortable delivery
Laughter only with humour
Voice tones stay even when making statement

Aggressive body language

Posture
Erect, tense, rigid
Shoulders back
Feet and legs shift around jerkily, or are planted in one place but with the chin up or thrust forward
Sitting with feet on desk and hands behind head, or tensely leaning forward

Gestures
Chopping or jabbing with hands
Clenched hands or pointing
Sweeping arms
Sharp, quick nods

Facial expression
Furrowed brow
Tight jaw and lips
Tense look, unblinking glare
Patronising or sarcastic smile
Shows anger with disapproving scowl, very firm mouth or bared teeth, extreme flush

Voice
Steely quiet or loud, harsh 'biting off' words
Precise measured delivery
Sarcastic laughter
Statements sound like orders or pronouncements, e.g. 'Do as you're told now!', 'Don't argue', 'That's my last word on the subject'

DO

Say 'no' politely and firmly e.g. 'No, thanks, I don't smoke'

Express feelings honestly e.g. 'I'm angry', 'I'm disappointed', 'I'm delighted', 'I enjoy being with you'

Be realistic, respectful and honest e.g. 'This is the third time you have been late when we agreed to meet and I feel cross with you'

Express preferences and priorities e.g. 'I don't have a particular film to suggest but I don't want to go to a very violent one'

DON'T

Deny responsibility for your choices e.g. 'I can't', 'I won't be able to'

De-personalise your feelings and deny ownership of your preferences e.g. 'You make me mad', 'That's disappointing', 'That's delightful', 'You make me feel so good'

Exaggerate, minimise or use sarcasm e.g. 'You are never on time', 'Uh, okay. We wouldn't want to strain your will power!'

Don't agree just to be sociable and don't agree unwillingly e.g. 'I don't care – whatever everyone else wants is okay with me'

	Person A	**Person B**	**Person C**
First roleplay	Speaker who will act in an assertive manner.	Listener who will act in either a passive or aggressive manner (own choice).	Observer who will give feedback to the others about what he or she saw happening in the roleplay.
Second roleplay	Observer who will give feedback to the others about what he or she saw happening in the roleplay.	Speaker who will act in an assertive manner.	Listener who will act in either a passive or aggressive manner (own choice).

Situations

1. Someone is telling you what time the buses to the nearest town leave. You did not understand what they have just told you and you want them to restate the information.

2. You have a Saturday job and you believe you deserve a pay rise. You decide to ask your boss directly.

3. Your parents have invited you to come to a social event with them that does not interest you. Decline the invitation!

4. You are pleased about what someone has done for you. For example, your sister has cleared out a space in the garage for your bike. Tell her how you feel.

RED LIGHTS

Receiving or noticing signals like those listed below will indicate when you are headed down the wrong road in your conversation with someone.

Have a look at the red light signals below and think about them. If you are in a situation later today or tomorrow when you notice yourself using one of them, STOP! It's OK to stop and say something like: 'Excuse me. Let me start again.' Other people will respect your efforts to communicate well. If you keep practising like this you will soon be able to avoid the red lights in your conversations with people most of the time.

- Saying 'you should', 'you must', 'you have to'. Restate as a request.
- Using exaggerated words such as 'obviously', 'absolutely', 'always', 'never', 'impossible'. Restate with more realistic and factual words.
- Saying 'y'know', 'maybe', 'kind of', 'sort of', 'only', 'just', 'I guess'. Restate in a more direct, confident manner without the wishy-washy qualifiers.
- Asking 'can you', 'could you', 'would you', 'why don't you', 'would you mind', 'do you think you might'. Request by asking 'will you please' because it is the only question that truly asks for action and a commitment.
- Using 'it', 'that', 'one', 'you', 'we' instead of 'I'. State your thoughts with 'I think', your opinions with 'I believe', and your feelings with 'I feel [mad, sad, glad, scared]' or 'I am [mad, sad, glad, scared]'.

GREEN LIGHTS

Receiving the following signals from other people indicates you are on the right track and communicating assertively. Keep going when you get green lights.

- When you feel relaxed, comfortable and stress-free. These are positive signs that you are being assertive.
- When the person with whom you are interacting displays attentiveness, comfort, co-operation and respect. When you see no signals of bad feelings, rebellion, disregard or defensiveness, you have chosen the best way to deal with that person.
- When another person says 'OK', 'sure' or 'I'll be glad to' in response to your request or directive.
- When others do what you wanted with no indication of resentment or discomfort, you have good evidence that you got your message over well.
- When others are assertive with you. When they communicate their honest thoughts, feelings, opinions, wants and needs in a direct and respectful manner, they are affirming your honest and direct behaviour with them.

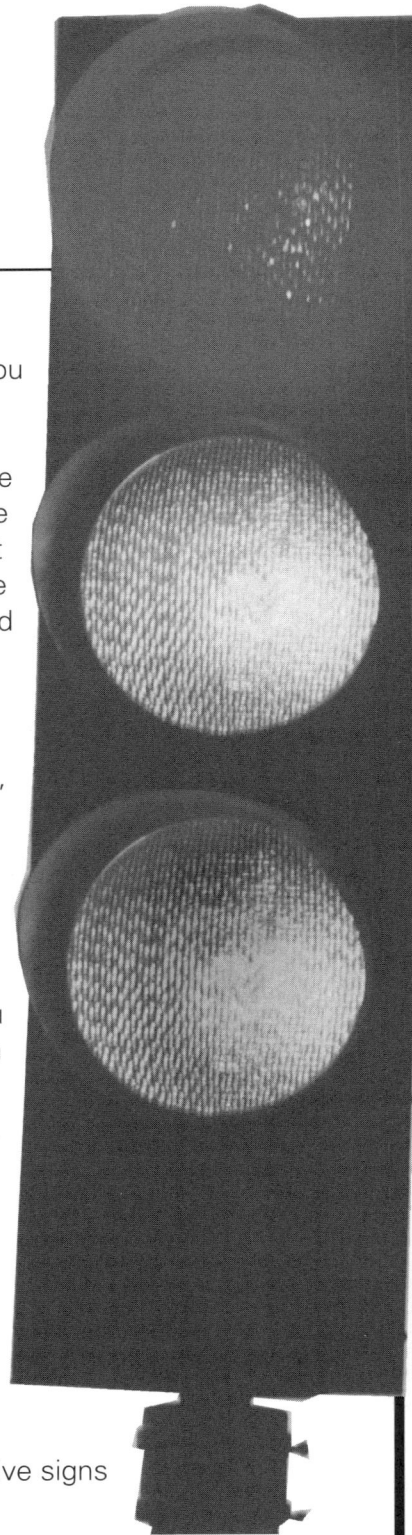

In threes, roleplay some of these situations using the techniques you have learnt.

Situation 1: Your friend has taken your favourite pen to write some notes and has forgotten to give it back to you. You ask for it back and she doesn't respond.

Situation 2: Your brother has told you he'll tell your mother that he has seen you smoking if you don't give him a fiver. You've asked him nicely not to do this and he isn't responding. What do you do next? What do you say next?

Situation 3: Your tutor has asked you to bring in photographs to use in one of your projects and after a couple of requests to your mother she has still not looked some out for you. What will you do and say now?

SELF-ESTEEM INDICATOR

- Self-Esteem Indicator: Secondary
- Scoring Overlay

Self-Esteem Indicator: Secondary

nferNelson
understanding potential

Student's name: .... Class: .... Age: ....

Administrator's name: .... Date: ....

Please answer all the questions. Circle the number to the right that you believe most accurately describes
the student's situation/response to each question.

	Most of the time	Quite often	Occasionally	Almost never
1. If this student is encouraged, does s/he respond positively?	3	2	1	0
2. Is this student co-operative in a group if something needs to be done or achieved?	3	2	1	0
3. Does this student usually enjoy and get on well with his/her work?	3	2	1	0
4. Does this student seem to be aware of what s/he is feeling (e.g. could this student tell you what s/he was feeling at any point in the day)?	3	2	1	0
5. Apart from you, does this student have significant adults who support and encourage him/her?	3	2	1	0
6. Does this student react reasonably if his/her schoolwork is constructively criticised?	3	2	1	0
7. Do you feel interested/excited when you think of this student, rather than worried or annoyed?	3	2	1	0
8. Do other students like him/her?	3	2	1	0
9. Does this student come over to you as being sure of him/herself?	3	2	1	0
10. Does this student seem to like being a boy/girl (e.g. gets on well with the same sex friends and joins in with the more stereotypical masculine or feminine activities fairly comfortably)?	3	2	1	0
11. Has this student always got plenty to say to other people?	3	2	1	0
12. Does this student make a plan before attempting a task?	3	2	1	0
13. Does this student like to imagine his/her future life in a positive way (e.g. think of essays or roleplays s/he has done)?	3	2	1	0
14. Does this student comfortably make social overtures to a new student?	3	2	1	0
15. Does this student try something first before giving up?	3	2	1	0
16. Can this student control his/her frustration and impatience?	3	2	1	0
17. Do other students often choose him/her to socialise with?	3	2	1	0
18. Is this student's reading and writing work at the right level for his/her age?	3	2	1	0
19. Does this student usually seem to be positive about things?	3	2	1	0
20. Does this student have any of the following – a best friend, a few close friends, a wide circle of friends?	3	2	1	0
21. Is this student independent, and does s/he like to do things his/her own way?	3	2	1	0
22. Is this student usually contented with his/her life?	3	2	1	0
23. Does this student seem to get on well with you and other significant adults?	3	2	1	0
24. Is this student's numeracy work at the right level for his/her age?	3	2	1	0
25. Does this student usually appear interested and curious about things and people?	3	2	1	0
26. Do you like this student?	3	2	1	0
27. Is this student reasonably competent at something s/he enjoys?	3	2	1	0
28. Is this student generally healthy?	3	2	1	0
29. Does this student initiate social activities relatively easily?	3	2	1	0
30. Can this student stand up for him/herself assertively rather than aggressively?	3	2	1	0

Overall self-esteem score ☐

Sense of self component score ☐

Sense of belonging component score ☐

Sense of personal power component score ☐

Scoring Overlay

Instructions for scoring the three components of self-esteem: To score sense of self, place the first column of this overlay over the completed Indicator ensuring that the item numbers line up. Sum the ratings for the circled responses to give a score for this component. Enter the score on the Indicator in the box provided. Score sense of belonging and sense of power in the same way.

Sense of self
Sense of belonging
Sense of personal power

Published by nferNelson Publishing Company Ltd, The Chiswick Centre, 414 Chiswick High Road, London W4 5TF, UK.

nferNelson is a division of Granada Learning Limited, part of Granada plc.